Balance With Blended Learning

What Your Colleagues Are Saying . . .

This book provides the fundamentals needed to transform your classroom from teacher centered to student centered. Catlin Tucker has thoroughly outlined the steps needed to create a blended learning environment with the necessary student–teacher partnership.

—**Kelly Fitzgerald**
Instructional Coach, Rouse High School
Leander, TX

After reading Balance With Blended Learning, *I was hooked! This new focus in the series, on helping coach students to understand their own learning, is exactly what educators need right now as we move from the front of the classroom to sitting shoulder to shoulder with our students to make sense of learning goals and assessing them!*

—**Melissa Wood-Glusac**
English Teacher, Thousand Oaks High School
Thousand Oaks, CA

Catlin Tucker has created a resource to help teachers better assess their students' work and more importantly, help students become more engaged in the process. Balance With Blended Learning: Partner With Your Students to Reimagine Learning and Reclaim Your Life *will undoubtedly help secondary teachers promote more student-friendly grading experiences that aid them in demonstrating their own progress and growth. It will help any teacher make changes to their assessment practices that will benefit student learning.*

—**Starr Sackstein**
Author, *Hacking Assessment*
Educational Consultant

As teachers, we strive to foster and nurture lifelong learners—learners that sustain their purpose and passion for learning regardless of their path in life. What Catlin shares with us in this book takes us one giant step forward toward that goal by focusing on grades and student ownership of their learning progression. Using her personal and very transparent experiences as a teacher, she unlocks a pathway for us to truly partner with our learners and thus move them closer to lifelong learning by actively involving them in monitoring their own learning progress. As a parent, teacher, and teacher educator, the ideas in this book will change the way I "do business" inside and outside of my classroom.

—John Almarode
Associate Professor of Education, College of Education
James Madison University

Balance With Blended Learning

Partner With Your Students to Reimagine Learning and Reclaim Your Life

Catlin R. Tucker

CORWIN

A SAGE Publishing Company

A SAGE Publishing Company

FOR INFORMATION:

Corwin

A SAGE Company

2455 Teller Road

Thousand Oaks, California 91320

(800) 233-9936

www.corwin.com

SAGE Publications Ltd.

1 Oliver's Yard

55 City Road

London EC1Y 1SP

United Kingdom

SAGE Publications India Pvt. Ltd.

B 1/I 1 Mohan Cooperative Industrial Area

Mathura Road, New Delhi 110 044

India

SAGE Publications Asia-Pacific Pte. Ltd.

18 Cross Street #10-10/11/12

China Square Central

Singapore 048423

Acquisitions Editor: Ariel Curry

Development Editor: Desirée A. Bartlett

Associate Content Development

  Editor: Jessica Vidal

Project Editor: Amy Schroller

Copy Editor: Lana Todorovic-Arndt

Typesetter: Hurix Digital

Proofreader: Sue Irwin

Indexer: Wendy Allex

Cover Designer: Gail Buschman

Marketing Manager: Margaret O'Connor

SUSTAINABLE FORESTRY INITIATIVE   Certified Sourcing   www.sfiprogram.org   SFI-00756

This book is printed on acid-free paper.

20 21 22 23 24 10 9 8 7 6 5 4 3 2 1

Table of Contents

Visit the companion website at
resources.corwin.com/balancewithBL
for downloadable resources.

.

Preface

There are two aspects of the teaching profession that I find incredibly draining: grading and communicating with parents. I know students need to receive regular feedback, so they know where they are excelling and where they need to focus their time and energy to improve. I also want to be clear that most parents are lovely and supportive, but there are always a handful of parents each year that are aggressive and demanding. Ironically, these two challenging aspects of my job—grades and parents—are often linked.

Parents are frustrated by what they perceive as a lack of communication from teachers about how their students are progressing. On the other side of this tension are teachers with anywhere from 30 to 150+ students. Many teachers are still employing a teacher-centric approach to their jobs. They deliver and facilitate lessons during the actual school day, but the rest of their responsibilities—designing learning experiences, grading student work, attending meetings, and communicating with parents—happen outside of the school day, invading their lives beyond school. It is exhausting and robs teachers of the time they need to relax and recharge.

Three years ago, I made two important decisions. First, I was not going to take grading home anymore. Second, I was going to have students track their progress and communicate directly with their parents on a regular basis. These two shifts changed my teaching reality and led me to re-evaluate (yet again) my role and my students' role in the classroom as well.

For the last 10 years, I've been using blended learning models and technology to shift control in the classroom from me to my students. However, it was not until I changed the way I approached feedback, assessment, and parent communication that I had an epiphany. Teachers must partner with their students! If teachers and students work together to assess, track, and reflect on the learning happening in the classroom, teachers will have the time and energy to innovate and personalize learning.

> If teachers and students work together to assess, track, and reflect on the learning happening in the classroom, teachers will have the time and energy to innovate and personalize learning.

The goal of this book is to provide teachers using blended learning models and technology with the resources, strategies, and tools necessary to partner with their students on assessment. Grades are not something that should happen *to* students. Grades and academic progress must be an ongoing, two-way conversation between the teacher and the learner. The more transparency we create around student progress, the more effectively students can take ownership of their learning and articulate that progress to their parents, keeping them in the learning loop.

I wrote this book primarily for secondary teachers; however, elementary teachers can take and adapt many of these principles, strategies, and ideas for their classrooms. Elementary teachers do not have as many students, and their students do not typically generate the same volume of work as secondary students, but teaching elementary students strategies that encourage them to be active and engaged learners will benefit them as they progress through school. Regardless of the grade level, teachers are drowning in work and need concrete strategies they can use to shift the traditional workflow in their classrooms to be more effective, efficient, and energized.

This book will present ideas and strategies that may initially feel lofty or unrealistic given your particular teaching assignment. I want to reassure you that I have done this in a public school with class sizes of approximately 30 students. It did not always go smoothly. It required time, practice, and fine tuning, but it worked. You don't need to do everything all at once. I certainly didn't. I would encourage teachers reading this book to try one strategy at a time. You will make mistakes, you will hit bumps, and then you will find a way to make it work for you.

My goal is to inspire a mind shift in the way teachers view both their role and responsibilities in the classroom as well as their students'. This is a process. It took me 4 years to get to the point where I was truly partnering with my students in our classroom. I hope that this book inspires teachers to approach their work in a more sustainable way that prioritizes their relationships with students. I am confident that the more of these strategies teachers can incorporate into their classrooms, the more rewarding they will find their work.

Acknowledgments

I want to say a special thank you to Katee Dean, Ely Jauregui, Karen Clancy-Cribby, Joanne Weatherby, Marisa Thompson, Heather Ellis, Carlyn Nichols, Jacquelyn Langdon, Nicholas A. Emmanuele, and Jeff Hennigar for lending their experience and voices to this book.

PUBLISHER'S ACKNOWLEDGMENTS

Corwin gratefully acknowledges the contributions of the following reviewers:

Kelly Fitzgerald
Instructional Coach
Rouse High School
Leander, TX

Melissa Wood-Glusac
English Teacher
Thousand Oaks High School
Thousand Oaks, CA

About the Author

 **Catlin R. Tucker** is a Google Certified Innovator, blended learning coach, best-selling author, international trainer, and keynote speaker who taught in Sonoma County for 16 years, where she was named Teacher of the Year in 2010. Catlin's books *Blended Learning in Grades 4–12* and *Blended Learning in Action* are both bestsellers designed to support teachers shifting to blended learning. Catlin's book *Power Up Blended Learning* provides school leaders and blended learning coaches with a clear path to create a profession learning infrastructure designed to maximize the effectiveness of blended learning on their campuses. Catlin is working on her doctorate at Pepperdine University. She is active on Twitter @Catlin_Tucker and writes an internationally ranked education blog at CatlinTucker.com.

This book is dedicated to Marika Neto, who inspired me, took risks with me, and challenged the status quo in education with me. I appreciate your friendship, your energy, and your willingness to push boundaries. Working with you has been one of the highlights of my teaching career. This book would not have been possible without you.

CHAPTER 1

The Problem With Traditional Grading Practices

"If a paper is returned with both a grade and a comment, many students will pay attention to the grade and ignore the comment."

—Susan Brookhart

For years, I did what most teachers do. I graded everything. I was like Oprah Winfrey, but instead of cars, I was giving away points. "You get points! And you get points! Everyone gets points!" Students received points for bringing their silent sustained reading books to class. They received points for annotating their nightly reading. They received points for completing classwork. I dumped hundreds of points into my digital grade book over the course of a semester. When grades were due, my online grade book spit out a percentage for each student, and that was the grade he or she received.

I remember feeling moments of unease as I reported grades. I had students who received *A*s because they did all of their work, but I knew they had not mastered grade-level skills. I also had students who earned low grades because they did not do their homework, yet they performed well on assessments. On some level, I knew my approach to grading wasn't an accurate reflection of my students' skills and abilities. Despite my unease, I was doing what I was taught to do in credential school and what I experienced as a student. The status quo is a powerful barrier to change.

> The status quo is a powerful barrier to change.

Not only did my approach to grading leave me questioning the accuracy of the grades I gave my students, but it also reinforced my students' myopic focus on the accumulation of points. Since everything they did had a point value, they were constantly asking me, "Tucker, how many points is this worth?" They were more concerned with earning points and less concerned about what those points reflected about their skills and abilities. This was my fault. I was sending the message that if you do the work, you get the points. This traditional approach to grading was exhausting and created a classroom culture focused on grades, not learning.

When I finally began to recognize the fundamental problems with my traditional approach to grading, I was able to make changes that freed me from the never-ending pile of paperwork I used to take home and to design a new approach to assessment and grading that was anchored in a partnership between me and my students. Instead of grades that rewarded compliance, I wanted to work *with* my students to ensure that grades reflected their mastery of skills.

Before most educators are willing to rethink something as fundamental as grading and assessment, it is helpful to acknowledge some of the myriad problems that exist with traditional grading practices.

PROBLEMS WITH TRADITIONAL GRADES

As I began to re-evaluate my approach to feedback, assessment, and grades, I began to see the flaws in the traditional grading practices I had been using for years.

1. Traditional grades did not reflect mastery of grade-level skills.

2. Traditional grades are used like carrots to get students to complete work.

3. Traditional grades put the focus on the product, not the process.

4. Traditional grading practices do not clearly align the grades entered into the grade book with specific skills.

5. Traditional grading practices do not provide an incentive for students to revisit and improve graded work.

6. Traditional grades do not require that students *think* about their learning.

7. Traditional grades happen *to* students.

Let's take a deeper look at some of these problems with traditional grades.

#1 Traditional Grades Do Not Reflect Mastery of Grade-Level Skills

Some students do well in school because they understand the game. They turn in all of their assignments and manage their time well. These students typically receive top marks for compliance, time management, and effort. However, compliance, time management, and effort are not the same as mastering grade-level content skills.

For years, I felt uncomfortable reporting grades because I knew my grades were rewarding academic habits more than they reflected my students' skills as English language arts students. I had students who received *A*s because they did everything I asked them to do, but I knew some of those students were not *A*-level students in terms of their skills. Conversely, I had students who received failing grades because they did not do the majority of classwork and homework, yet they performed well on assessments. This disconnect between my students' abilities and their class grades caused me to feel uneasy when submitting grades.

When I finally transitioned to a standards-based approach to assessment, I had several tough conversations with students about their grades and what those grades reflected about their skills. I had students who had always received *A*s and expected to continue doing so in my class. When we looked through their body of work during our grade interviews (covered in Chapter 11), scores hovered between 2.5 and 3 out of 4 on most skills. They didn't like hearing that they were not receiving an *A* because they had not demonstrated mastery of grade-level skills. These conversations were hard, and often emotional, for kids used to traditional grading practices. My students had been conditioned to believe that if they turned in all of the work, they would receive an *A*. Even though these conversations were tough, they motivated students to begin thinking about how they could develop their skills. Students began to seek me out asking for support because they wanted to improve specific skills. Shifting to a standards-based approach to grading effectively shifted the conversation from grades to learning. Those are the conversations I *want* to have with students.

#2 Traditional Grades Are Used Like Carrots to Get Students to Complete Work

In my role as a blended learning coach and professional development facilitator, I hear teachers frequently making statements like, "Well, if I don't grade it, students won't do it." I understand this fear, but it only reinforces traditional grading practices and keeps the focus on points. We must create a classroom culture in which students recognize the value of the work they do. I believe that if students understand the purpose of the work they are doing, are able to appreciate their growth and progress, enjoy agency, and feel the work is stimulating and relevant to their lives, they *will* do it.

In Daniel Pink's (2009) book *Drive: The Surprising Truth about What Motivates Us*, the author specifically calls out grades. He equates grades with metaphorical carrots, used to reward compliance even though they rarely provide an accurate picture of what students have learned. Pink highlights the damage that grades can do to a student's motivation when they don't do well. Grades can kill motivation by making those students who receive zeros for missing work or *D*s and *F*s for incomplete or incorrect work feel they are not good enough. Instead of sending the message that failure is a natural part of the learning process, failure becomes scary, shameful, and something to avoid at all costs. If students do not feel there is space to fail, they will stop taking risks.

The problem with assigning a point value to every task or assignment is that grades reflect work habits, organizational skills, and motivation as much if not more than they reflect skill levels. Students who bring their supplies, do all of their homework, and participate in the class receive a lot of points and typically do well in school. I'm not suggesting that there isn't value in learning these important life skills, but it is important to be honest about what we are grading and what the motivation is behind giving those grades. Are we using grades to assess skills, or are we using them to punish students who don't do the work we have assigned?

Rethinking traditional grading practices and partnering with students on assessment can change the culture around grades to create a natural incentive for students to *want* to complete work to improve their skills.

#3 Traditional Grades Place the Focus on the Product, Not the Process

Traditional grades emphasize the product, not the process. Teachers assign work. Students often complete that work in isolation. Then teachers collect that work and grade it in isolation. There is not enough class time dedicated to providing students with feedback as they work. In part, I believe this is a result of the pressure teachers feel to cover content in class. Teachers using traditional teacher-led instructional models spend a lot of time introducing new information and don't feel they have the time to sit with students and provide feedback in class.

When I was using a whole-group teacher-led model, I spent our in-class time presenting the *how*. I wanted students to understand how to solve a problem or complete a specific type of writing, but I did not allocate time in class to support them as they worked. Instead, I spent 90% of my energy assessing finished products and only about 10% of my time providing feedback during the process. Now, I do the opposite. I spend 90% of my time supporting the process by providing real-time feedback and conferencing with students as they work and only about 10% of my time assessing their finished products. It is a much more rewarding experience to focus on the process because it yields a higher-quality product.

#4 Traditional Grades Do Not Clearly Align the Grades Entered Into the Grade Book With Specific Skills

Although many teachers use rubrics to assess student work and evaluate specific skills demonstrated in a single assignment, the grade they report is often an average of those individual skills. For example, an English teacher may grade several different aspects of a *Lord of the Flies* argumentative essay. He might evaluate the claims, evidence, analysis, and mechanics individually, but what most students and parents see when they look at an online grade book is a lump sum, like 81/100 on their essay.

Similarly, in science, students may be asked to build a model to demonstrate Newton's Third Law and write an explanation of their model. Instead of entering each part of this assignment separately focusing on the specific skills necessary to construct the model versus the skills required to write a cogent explanation, many teachers enter the two parts of this assignment as a single grade in the grade book. Unfortunately, that makes it challenging for students and their parents to understand what they did well and what they need to work on. The model may have been strong, while the explanation may have lacked detail and clarity. If the teacher assesses the individual skills employed to complete each part of the assignment and enters them as separate scores in the grade book, that creates more clarity about the student's areas of strength and weakness.

When teachers enter a single score that combines the average of several skills, it does not provide students or their parents with insight into what the child needs to focus on improving. As a result, parents and students tracking grades online may not understand exactly why the student earned a particular score or what skills that student should spend time and energy practicing.

When individual scores for each skill assessed are entered as separate items in a grade book, it creates transparency about which skills students are excelling at and which skills they need to work on. For example, the teacher entering scores for the *Lord of the Flies* argumentative essay can enter each element as a separate score in the grade book. Entering a score for each element of the assignment, as pictured below, makes it clear which skills the student is doing well on and which skills need additional practice and improvement.

Lord of the Flies argumentative essay: Claims = 3/4

Lord of the Flies argumentative essay: Evidence = 2/4

Lord of the Flies argumentative essay: Analysis = 1.5/4

Lord of the Flies argumentative essay: Mechanics = 3/4

The science teacher evaluating the model demonstrating Newton's Third Law and subsequent explanation of that model can identify the specific skills evident in the two parts of this assignment and enter those separately. Some students will excel at the model, while others may excel at the written explanation.

Newton's Third Law: Model applies scientific principle = 3.5/4

Newton's Third Law: Model presents a solution = 3/4

Newton's Third Law: Explanation includes strong evidence to support analysis = 2.5/4

Newton's Third Law: Describes the scientific principles present in the model = 2/4

To add to the confusion, many teachers separate their grade books into categories and assign each category a percentage of the overall grade. Homework might be 20% of a student's overall grade, while projects may constitute 10% of their grade. If students only do one project during a given grading period, that single score could have a dramatic impact on their overall grade in the class. This can cause anxiety, confusion, and frustration for students. Grades and grade books should clearly communicate what students are doing well and what they need to work on. If they don't accomplish this goal, grading practices and reporting need to change to ensure the grade book is user-friendly for students and parents.

#5 Traditional Grading Practices Do Not Provide an Incentive to Revisit and Improve Graded Work

Teachers invest massive amounts of time and energy grading finished products, and as a result, most teachers do not allow students to revise, edit, and resubmit their work for a new assessment score. They simply don't have time to re-assess student work. However, if there is no opportunity to take the feedback a teacher provides and improve work, then what is the purpose of the teacher's comments on the final product?

If teachers grade less, focus on providing feedback *as* students work, and allow students more agency in the grading and assessment process, we can create an incentive for students to continually revisit, revamp, and improve their work. Continual improvement should be the primary goal of every classroom, but grading practices must invite and encourage students to revisit and revise their work.

> If teachers grade less, focus on providing feedback *as* students work, and allow students more agency in the grading and assessment process, we can create an incentive for students to continually revisit, revamp, and improve their work.

#6 Traditional Grades Do Not Require Students to Think About Their Learning

Grading and assessment are one of the most time-consuming aspects of a teacher's job. Teachers feel intense pressure to stay on top of each child's progress and know where they are in terms of their learning at all times. That is a herculean task. Ironically, students are rarely asked to evaluate their work and reflect on what it reveals about their learning. That's a missed opportunity. The teacher cannot be the only person thinking about the students' learning. Students should be thinking metacognitively about their learning and what their work reflects about their content knowledge and skills.

Teachers who build metacognitive practices into their daily and weekly classroom routines will help students be active agents in their learning. Students *should* be asked to think about, reflect on, and track their work, progress, and learning. It is only when students take the time to look at their work and analyze their skills that they will appreciate the value of the work they do and understand where they are in their journey toward mastering specific skills. I realize teaching students to develop metacognitive skills takes time, and most teachers already feel they don't have enough time. However, building a metacognitive reflective practice into our classes can help our students take ownership of their learning by setting learning goals for themselves and tracking their progress toward those goals.

#7 Traditional Grades Happen *to* Students

Like too many aspects of education, students play a passive role in the traditional grading system. Students submit work. The teacher assesses the work and enters a score into a grade book. Then the teacher passes graded work back to students, and they are left to digest the grades and comments in isolation. In an alarming number of classrooms, the grade a student receives on an assignment is final. They don't have the opportunity to go back and edit, revise, or improve their work for a higher score. Teachers often cite their overwhelming workloads as the reason they cannot allow students to resubmit work. Unfortunately, that traditional workflow leaves students in a powerless position. If they don't get it right the first time, they are stuck with that grade. Given this reality, it shouldn't surprise anyone that students are tempted to cheat when they get stuck or experience high levels of anxiety at school.

Classrooms must be places where failure is embraced and trying again is encouraged. Learning is a process. Learning often involves making mistakes, but in many classrooms, students are not afforded this luxury. When grades are viewed as final, and students do not have agency in relation to their grades, it negatively impacts motivation and causes unnecessary stress.

In addition, the grades students receive on their report cards are often a surprise. Even teachers who use online grade books can fall into the trap of grading several large assignments right before grades are due, which can have a dramatic impact on a student's final grade. Grades shouldn't be a surprise. Grades and individual progress should be an ongoing conversation between the teacher and student. If there isn't transparency surrounding the grading and assessment process, students won't understand how to improve their skills or advocate for themselves as learners.

> Grades shouldn't be a surprise. Grades and individual progress should be an ongoing conversation between the teacher and student.

MY WHY

These problems with traditional grading practices serve as my WHY. They are the reason I decided to change my grading practices and partner with my students on assessment. Not only was my traditional approach to grading unsatisfying and unsustainable, but it did not foster a classroom culture in which students were free to be curious, take risks, experiment, and fail. Quite the opposite, traditional grading practices inspire fear and anxiety or loathing and apathy that limit learning. If students do not feel they have control over their learning or agency in the assessment process, they are less likely to be motivated and engaged in the learning.

> Not only was my traditional approach to grading unsatisfying and unsustainable, but it did not foster a classroom culture in which students were free to be curious, take risks, and experiment.

Teachers are also buckling under the pressure of traditional grading practices. In training sessions, when I ask teachers what their top pain points are, "time," "grading," and "student apathy" top the list. Teachers are exhausted. Many don't feel that the time they spend grading student work results in dramatic improvement, which is defeating. We need a new path—one grounded in a partnership model where the teacher and the students work together to ensure that feedback and assessment are valuable and help students progress as learners.

GRADES ARE HOTLY DEBATED IN EDUCATION

I am far from the only person in education frustrated with traditional grading practices. Many voices, including Mark Barnes, author of *Assessment 3.0: Throw Out Your Grade Book and Inspire Learning* (2015), advocate for tossing out grades in favor of authentic feedback and conversations about student progress. Barnes references the research of Alfie Kohn, who has made waves in education by criticizing traditional grading practices and the use of grades and rewards as detrimental to learning. In addition to the problems I've highlighted, Kohn (2016) says grades negatively impact learning because:

1. Grades decrease student interest. "Learning for a grade" isn't an effective motivator. Attaching a grade to work encourages a mentality of "do enough to get the *A*," which incorrectly suggests that learning has an end point.

2. Grades act as a deterrent to stretching or challenging oneself. If something is going to be graded, students want to be as successful as possible and will often select easier tasks.

3. Grades encourage shallow thinking. Students become myopically focused on what they need to know for a test instead of learning because they are passionate about or interested in a topic.

4. Anything that isn't graded feels unimportant. In that context, the teacher decides what gets graded, or what is important, and students lose all agency in the learning process. Instead, students must focus energy on teacher-designated information and tasks to get the highest grade possible.

Kohn (2016) points out that grades are used to "compel students to do stuff that they have little interest in doing," so the goal becomes compliance. *Compliance* is one of my *least favorite* words used in education. If our goal as educators is to get students to comply, we are unlikely to inspire a love of learning. Yes, students need to follow classroom protocols, be respectful, and work to improve their skills, but the word *compliance* implies a lack of power. In their research on self-determination, Deci and Ryan (1985) found that an individual's intrinsic motivation increases in situations where they experience autonomy and agency (Ryan, 1991). When the focus in a classroom is on compliance, students lose that agency, which negatively impacts their motivation as a learner. Compliance should not be our goal. Our goal should be to cultivate curious, capable, and creative thinkers and learners.

Kohn (2016) believes that the best teachers are the ones who "help students forget that grades exist" and in some cases "allow students to pick their own grades." In her book, *Hacking Assessment: 10 Ways to Go Gradeless in a Traditional Grades School*, Starr Sackstein (2015) encourages teachers who are required to report grades to "put the power of grading into the students' hands" (p. 109). Since grades are subjective and don't always provide an accurate reflection of a student's skills, Sackstein makes the argument that students should be actively involved in evaluating their work in relation to a clear set of standards. I absolutely agree that students need to play an active role in evaluating, tracking, reflecting on, and determining their grades in a class. This book is designed to help teachers using blended learning models to create time and space to shift grading practices so that students are actively involved in the assessment process.

IF WE CANNOT THROW OUT GRADES COMPLETELY, WHAT CAN WE DO?

In a perfect world, there would be no grades. But we don't live in a perfect world. Most of us do not have control over whether or not we have a grade book. Some schools even require teachers enter a specific number of grades into their online grade books each week. Teachers navigate a lot of mandates that can leave *us* feeling powerless.

Although there are educators and schools exploring grade free or nearly gradeless models, as evidenced in Jeff Henninger's vignette, this book does not demand that teachers throw out grades entirely because they probably don't have that luxury. For those teachers without the freedom to eliminate grades, I want to provide concrete strategies, tools, resources, and routines they can use to build a classroom culture that values learning over the accumulation of points, makes students active agents in the learning and assessment process, and encourages a partnership model between the teacher and the student.

So, even though we may not have the luxury of ditching grades entirely, we can build routines and norms that move feedback and assessment into the classroom, so learning becomes an ongoing conversation between the teacher and student.

Jeff Hennigar
Grade 5 teacher at BLT Senior Elementary School
Halifax, Nova Scotia, Canada
@MrHennigar

After a lot of reading about motivation and intrinsic/extrinsic rewards last year, I decided that I needed to go gradeless. I related to the authors and research as I reflected on how students negatively react to seeing graded assignments and tests. I promote an attitude of growth and progress with my students, and I needed my grading practices to reflect this. Throughout the year, I ran a near-gradeless program; report cards were the only communication of grades to the students. Assessments were either returned with single-point rubrics, written feedback, or followed up with a conference.

At the end of school this year, I met with each student in my fifth-grade class to discuss what fair grades would be for their report card. It was my first time using grade interviews with learners in my class. The interviews were focused on literacy and math, which are the subjects that are formally reported on in my province in upper-elementary. To prepare for the interviews, the students reviewed their work, completed reflections, and reviewed past feedback so they would have evidence to refer to. I also had notes written and an idea of what a fair grade could be before the interview. We do a lot of project-based learning in my classroom, so during independent reading and while students were working on things such as passion projects or creating carnival games using probability in math class, I made time to meet with each student for a 5–10-minute conversation.

Feedback and conferences are a big part of running a successful gradeless program, so meeting with me in private is a regular occurrence in our learning community. I let students take the lead during these conversations. When they needed prompts, I asked them to share the work they are proud of, or about something that they found challenging during the term. While discussing the actual grades, I discovered that 10-year-olds knew what success looked like. No one tried to get themselves all As (even the learners that ended up getting them). I never had to justify giving a lower grade, but several students did get higher grades than they were asking for based on my evidence and rationale. They felt the process was fair and worthwhile.

Removing the focus on grades shifts students' focus to other things. When the learning activities are relevant and engaging, their focus is shifted from doing things "good enough" to doing awesome work. Grades act like a ceiling for success; if you can get the A, you don't need to work any harder. By removing grades and focusing on growth and improvement, everyone has the same goal and we can learn from each other. It creates a classroom culture with less competition and spotlights the strengths that every learner in the room possesses. It has been a worthwhile shift of focus!

The challenge is that many teachers are trapped in a traditional teaching role. They plan whole group lessons that dedicate substantial time to the transfer of information and demand that they guide students through each part of the lesson. They spend their days facilitating lessons and rarely have the time and space to sit next to students as they work to provide them with real-time feedback, let alone conduct side-by-side assessment conversations, and conference with students about their goals and progress. Instead, they take home stacks (physical and virtual) of student work and labor for hours in the evenings and on weekends providing feedback on finished products. However, grading at home is energy sapping and robs teachers of the time they need to relax, recharge, and connect with their families.

BLENDED LEARNING TO THE RESCUE

Blended learning models offer teachers a much-needed opportunity to reimagine lesson design and facilitation to create the time and space they need to shift feedback and assessment into the classroom, while also encouraging students to take an active role in assessing their progress as learners.

At its core, blended learning is a shift in control from teacher to learner. The goal of the various blended learning models is to give students more agency over the time, place, pace, and path of their learning. As teachers embrace different blended learning models and leverage technology strategically, they realize they no longer need to stand in front of the class and orchestrate lessons. They can design lessons that allow students to drive the learning and create space for the teacher to support individual students or small groups of students as they work.

The "problems" associated with traditional grading practices discussed in this chapter can be alleviated if teachers use blended learning models to rethink their approach to lesson design and partner with their students on assessment. This book is written to support teachers using blended learning to shift the workflow in their classrooms and embrace grading practices that are sustainable, foster a partnership between the teacher and student, and encourage students to take an active role in tracking, assessing, and reflecting on their learning.

BOOK STUDY QUESTIONS

1. What aspects of your job are most challenging? What hurdles make it hard to teach and reach all students?

2. When and where do you typically assess student work? Do you involve students in the feedback and assessment process? Why, or why not?

3. How many hours outside of class do you spend grading in a typical week? If you did not have to spend that time grading, what would you enjoy doing with your time?

4. How effective do you feel traditional grading practices are in helping students to develop skills? Do you feel the time you invest in grading yields significant improvements in the quality of your students' work?

5. Which problem with traditional grading practices identified in this chapter resonated most with you? Why?

6. If you could add an additional problem to the list presented in this chapter, what would you add? How has this additional "problem" with

traditional grades impacted your teaching? What impact has it had on student learning and motivation?

7. How is your grade book organized? Do you use categories and percentages? If so, how might this impact a student's ability to track his or her progress? Does your grade book make it clear what skills the student is doing well on and which skills require more time and practice?

8. Do you encourage students to reflect on or track their progress in your class? If so, what does that process look like? How much class time do you dedicate to that practice? What are the benefits of building this practice into class?

9. Do you allow students to edit, revise, and reassess to improve work that has already been graded? If so, how do you manage this? What are the expectations for students? If you do not allow students to revisit prior work, what is driving that policy?

10. How do you think moving feedback and assessment into the classroom might impact your students' motivation and the overall class culture?

11. How do you feel about the argument that grades in any form are damaging and should be tossed out? Is that a conversation worth having at your school? What might some of the arguments against getting rid of grades be?

CHAPTER 2

Embracing a Partnership Model With Blended Learning

"The humanist, revolutionary educator's . . . efforts must be imbued with a profound trust in people and their creative power. To achieve this, they must be partners of the students in their relations with them."

—Paulo Freire

I began teaching when I was 22 years old. That first year, I walked into my classroom believing that

- The teacher possessed the knowledge.

- Students should sit in rows.

- A quiet classroom was an effective classroom.

- Students in the same class should complete the same assignments.

- Students would demonstrate their learning using pen and paper.

- It was my job to grade everything.

These initial assumptions about teaching and learning were grounded in my own experience as a student and were reinforced in my credential program, and these mental models informed my decision making early on in my teaching career. Unsurprisingly, I failed to create the classroom I had imagined while studying to be a teacher.

I realize now after years of attempting to unlearn everything I thought I knew about teaching that students don't want to learn in a space where they do not have any control. I was treating my classroom like a hierarchy, with me at the top with all of the knowledge and control. Students were at the bottom, and I expected them to sit quietly, listen, and complete the tasks I assigned. No wonder my students didn't want to engage with me, the content, or each other. I wish my experience was unique, but I fear that many teachers still run their classrooms in a top-down fashion that disenfranchises learners.

FROM HIERARCHY TO PARTNERSHIP

Traditionally, students have inhabited a relatively powerless position in the classroom. They are expected to comply with the teacher's directives. This hierarchical structure in the classroom creates tension between teachers and their students, which manifests in power struggles, classroom management issues, and decreased levels of intrinsic motivation. The problem lies in the fact that this classic power structure denies students agency and autonomy. Autonomy, or the freedom to control one's actions, has been identified as a basic human need that, when met, yields higher levels of intrinsic motivation and improves learning outcomes (Deci & Ryan, 1985; Deci & Ryan, 1991).

Instead of thinking of our relationship with students as hierarchical, we should think of ourselves as partners working with our students to customize learning to best meet their needs. Students will experience more academic success if they take an active role in articulating their goals, identifying their needs and interests, reflecting on their growth, and advocating for themselves as learners. Blended learning models, unlike traditional teacher-led instruction, can provide teachers and students with the time and space to nurture this partnership.

Blended learning models are designed to give students more control over their learning, while creating opportunities for teachers to provide personalized instruction, support, scaffolding, and feedback. If teachers are willing to relinquish control, prioritize student agency, and commit to partnering with learners, the transition to blended learning has the potential to be transformative.

Blended learning models offer educators a way to reimagine instructional design and facilitation with the goal of creating a student-centered learning environment and personalizing learning experiences for individual students

(Patrick, Kennedy, & Powell, 2013). Blended learning does not equate personalized learning, but it does offer educators a path toward personalization if they partner with their students.

PARTNERSHIP PRINCIPLES FOR TEACHERS AND STUDENTS

Forming a partnership is easier to do if the partnership is grounded in clear principles. The principles below are inspired, in part, by the work of Jim Knight, who articulated partnership principles to guide an instructional coaching relationship, as well as my work as an educator, blended learning coach, and doctoral student.

As shown in Figure 2.1, a truly successful teacher–student partnership must

1. Be built on mutual respect and trust
2. Have a shared purpose

FIGURE 2.1 Partnership Principles for Teachers and Students

3. Be grounded in reciprocity

4. Prioritize open and honest communication

5. Rely on regular feedback to improve

6. Balance power to ensure each partner has an equal voice and choice

7. Be committed to learning together

Built on Mutual Respect and Trust

In one of my favorite TED Talks on education titled "Every Kid Needs a Champion," Rita Pierson (2013) makes the point that learning is grounded in relationships. Her words echo the sentiments of earlier humanistic educators who viewed students as people first and learners second. The humanistic approach does not separate the cognitive from the affective, but instead, it aims to teach and reach the whole child (Khatib, Sarem, & Hamidi, 2013). To do this effectively, educators must form meaningful relationships with their students. Forming relationships with students is a fundamental component of a person-centered approach to education. Students need to feel like they have a meaningful connection with their teachers if they are going to lean into learning, which means teachers would do well to begin forming those relationships on the first day of school. As tempting as it is to dive into curriculum because we have so much to cover, building relationships with our students and establishing respectful routines should come first.

Learning requires that students take risks, experiment, and fail. Students need to feel safe and supported if they are to embrace the inherent vulnerability that comes with learning something new. Students are more willing to take risks if they respect and trust their teachers. The most famous line from Pierson's TED Talk is "kids don't learn from people they don't like." Students know when teachers care about them because they make time to connect with them and understand them. Making a personal connection with every child is easier to do if teachers spend less time talking at the front of the room and more time sitting with small groups or individual students supporting them as they work. When teachers have conversations with students, listen to their questions and respond thoughtfully, ask for their opinions, and allow them a voice and choice in the class, students feel respected and valued, and as a result, they are more likely to learn.

Even though I feel pressure to jump into curriculum, I spend the first few weeks of school "onboarding" students. We spend time practicing classroom routines, engaging in team building activities, getting to know one another, and establishing norms for our interactions on and offline. On the first day of class, students rotate through four separate stations pictured in Figure 2.2. The lesson is designed to introduce them to the Station Rotation Model and shift the focus from me to them.

FIGURE 2.2 First Day of Class Station Rotation Lesson

Station 1: Online Time to Take a Selfie Icebreaker	Students take a selfie, post it to a Padlet Wall, and answer a series of questions. • Where is your happy place? • Do you consider yourself an introvert, an extrovert, or a mix? • What is one thing you wish you had more time for in your life? • What do you do to relax? • What is something you like about yourself?
Station 2: Offline Read and Annotate the Syllabus	Students read the syllabus and make notes about the important information. After they read the syllabus, they write at least one question they have about the class on a sticky note and put it on the wall. At the end of class, I circle back to answer their questions.
Station 3: Online Google Form Student Survey	Students complete a survey with questions about their parents' contact information (e.g., email address) and primary language spoken at home. The survey includes questions about their previous experiences in school (e.g., favorite subject, a time they failed and how they reacted, a moment when they experienced success). I ask if they enjoy reading and writing and invite them to explain. I include questions about their access to and feelings about technology. The Google Form is extensive, but the information students share is invaluable.
Station 4: Offline Tucker Time	When students are at my station, I ask them to first create a name card they can put on their desks so I can immediately begin learning their names. Once they all have a name card, and once I've noted their names on my roll sheet, I ask them to pair up and interview their partner using the following five questions: • How would you describe yourself as a student? • What is your greatest strength and what is your greatest weakness? • What are you most looking forward to in this class? • What are you most nervous about? • What is one thing you hope to accomplish this year? As students interview each other, I observe and attempt to commit their names to memory. When they are done, I introduce our first writing assignment which is called the "random autobiography." It is a poem composed of random bits of information about the students' lives. By way of introduction, I read my random autobiography for them, and then they begin to work on their own.

My goal with this first-day Station Rotation lesson is to communicate to students that I care about who they are as individuals and that I want to get to know them, so I can make sure our class will be interesting and relevant for them.

Shared Purpose

Traditionally, it has been the teacher's responsibility to define the purpose of a lesson or unit, identify learning goals, and design assessments to measure whether or not students have achieved those goals. This traditional workflow does not invite students into the process. Instead, it requires that teachers do the lion's share of the work. In Chapter 3, I will talk about how the teacher's tendency to do the work in the classroom limits their innovative potential and robs students of opportunities to drive their learning.

In a partnership model, people work together to define the purpose of the work they do. If students are going to appreciate the potential value of their work, they must understand the purpose of that work. That is easier to do if they are asked to help articulate *why* they are doing what they are doing in the classroom. For example, some assignments are designed to allow students the opportunity to practice skills, while others are designed to assess skills. Unfortunately, the purpose of the work students do is often unclear, so the motivating factor of the assignment is not the intrinsic value of that work, but rather the extrinsic grade that teachers attach to the assignment. Unfortunately, extrinsic motivators are much less effective long-term than intrinsic motivators (Pink, 2009). Over time, students become myopically focused on the accumulation of points instead of on the purpose and value of the work they are doing. This is a trend I hope educators can combat by partnering with students to think about and define the purpose of the work they are doing in the classroom.

Helping students to understand, appreciate, and articulate the purpose of the work they do is easier to accomplish if students are actively engaged in setting learning goals. Learning goals, as opposed to performance goals, are associated with a mastery-oriented mindset and place the focus on improving and developing skills (Dweck & Leggett, 1988; Heyman & Dweck, 1992). When students set learning goals, they begin to think more consciously about what they need to do to meet those goals. What additional instruction, practice, or support do they need to continue developing? As a result, they begin to think about the purpose of tasks and assignments through the lens of their journey toward mastering specific skills. In Chapter 5, I will review what learning goals are, present two strategies students can use to think about and set their learning goals, and explain how the practice of setting and revisiting goals can help students to develop a mastery mindset and increase their intrinsic motivation.

In addition to the practice of setting goals, this book presents several different strategies designed to invite students into the process of thinking about, reflecting on, and articulating the purpose of the work they do. In Chapter 4, we will discuss metacognitive strategies teachers can incorporate into their classrooms to encourage students to regularly reflect on their learning.

Grounded in Reciprocity

In a partnership, both sides must be willing to give and receive time, energy, and respect. Both parties in a partnership—teacher and learner—should benefit and grow from the experience of working together. Friesen (2008) asserts that "authentic intellectual engagement requires a deeper reciprocity in the teaching–learning relationship where students' engagement begins as they actively construct their learning in partnership with teachers" (p. 8). When teachers form a partnership with their students and invite students to take an active role shaping their learning experiences, that partnership positively impacts student engagement.

I feel the reciprocity in my partnership with students most when we work through student-designed projects. When my students work on a project, I carve out time in class regularly to meet with groups. Typically, I provide a big umbrella topic, like sustainability, mental health, or social media. Then students identify an aspect of that large topic that they want to focus on, form a group of similarly interested peers, pitch a project proposal, and work through the five stages of the design thinking process: empathize, define, ideate, prototype, and test.

It's during the different stages of a project when I feel like I am challenged to learn and grow right alongside my students. They need me to help them define the scope of their projects, connect with stakeholders and professionals with expertise on the issue, maintain momentum when the project feels overwhelming or stagnant, and publish for an authentic audience. This practice of working directly with students to guide them in constructing their learning is an intellectually challenging, engaging, and rewarding endeavor.

When teachers commit to partnering with their students and carve out time to engage them in conversations about their interests, needs, and challenges, it does not take long to realize that the traditional one-size-fits-all approach to teaching is inadequate to meet the diverse needs of all students. Instead of developing one lesson for the whole class, teachers should draw on their experiences and expertise to support individual learners in articulating a learning path that is both rigorous and relevant. This is a challenging and intellectually stimulating exercise for teachers.

Prioritize Honest and Open Communication

Open and honest communication is the cornerstone of any strong relationship, and that includes the teacher–student relationship. However, the traditional design of most classrooms does not afford teachers the time to engage in conversations with individual students. Class periods fly by in a rush of activity, teachers spend large portions of time speaking to the entire class, and students are not often afforded the opportunity to share their thoughts.

These traditional barriers to conversation make it challenging for educators to understand and connect with learners. This is unfortunate, because teachers are tasked with teaching diverse groups of students, and without time to talk, how can we possibly know what individual learners need to be successful?

When conversations do happen, they tend to be one-sided with the teacher talking and the student listening. It is important for teachers to make time to check in with students and listen to their thoughts, questions, and concerns. This is the easiest way to find out what students are understanding and where they need additional support.

In an analysis of J. F. Herbart's work on listening, Andrea English (2011) says that

> each individual learner is unique and can only be understood by the teacher in the moment, that is, through lived experiences and interpersonal interaction; the individual must 'be discovered, not deduced' . . . this means that the teachers must understand both *where the learner is starting from* in his or her learning process, and *where the learner still needs to go.* (p. 180; emphasis in original)

It's interesting that Herbart, who was writing about education in the early 1800s, essentially made an argument for personalizing learning through the act of listening. He notes that the only way to know where each learner is and effectively meet individual students where they are is to listen critically. Teachers should design lessons that allow them to engage in conversation with individual students with the goal of understanding their unique needs and perspectives. This will make it possible to design instruction, scaffolds, and practice that will meet their specific needs.

My favorite moments with students take place when we sit down and talk. I periodically dedicate my teacher-led station to question and answer sessions or informal check-ins. Some teachers might view this as a waste of precious instructional minutes, but it does two things. One, it communicates to students that I care enough about them to check-in and ask how they are doing. Two, based on these conversations, I can make adjustments that will improve their experience in class.

Conferencing, which is not something I did before embracing blended learning, is another powerful way to incorporate honest, open, and individualized conversations into the classroom. Using blended learning models, like the Whole Group Rotation and the Playlist, can allow teachers to pull individual students to conference, while the rest of the class is engaged in a blended, student-paced lesson. In Chapter 9, I'll make a case for the value of side-by-side assessments, which emphasize the importance of conversations about student progress as opposed to simply relying on written feedback or entering points in a grade book.

Rely on Regular Feedback to Improve the Partnership

In addition to open communication, partners need to provide one another with feedback. In Chapter 7, I introduce a strategy teachers can use to move feedback into the classroom with the goal of making feedback a regular part of the students' experience in class. Too often, feedback comes after work has been completed and does not help the student to improve the quality of the work *before* it is due and formally assessed. One major goal of this book is to help teachers rethink when, where, and why they provide students with feedback. Feedback is a powerful learning tool, but it must be used effectively to support students *as* they work.

Conversely, teachers need to invite feedback from their students to gain a complete understanding of how students feel about their experience in the classroom. Even though most teachers acknowledge the value of providing regular feedback to their students, teachers rarely ask for feedback in return. I have always found this odd. Students are essentially the customers in education. They consume what teachers dish out. Isn't it logical that we should check in with students to see how they feel about the instructional strategies, technology tools, and classroom routines we are using?

I wonder, does the hesitation to check in with students and request feedback stem from the teacher's insecurity or fears about what students will say? Are teachers afraid that students will say something negative about the way they are doing their jobs? I can understand this feeling. It taps into our vulnerability. That said, we often provide students with feedback that is critical. They have to process that feedback, make adjustments, and improve. I would argue that teachers should do the same.

For years, I have ended each semester with a class evaluation, which I create using a Google Form. I ask students to tell me which books they enjoyed most and least. I ask them which classroom routines were most and least helpful and which online tasks they enjoyed most and least. I remember, 3 years ago, I was reading through their responses and feeling defensive because so many students had identified annotations as a routine they did not enjoy. I have always felt that annotating is the best way to actively engage with a text so that students understand and remember what they read. When so many students made negative comments about our annotation routine, I was forced to take a step back and think about why I was pushing what worked for me onto my students. Ultimately, I decided to present three strategies for engaging with a text: traditional annotations, dialogic journal, and sketchnotes. The next semester, I allowed my students to choose the active reading strategy that worked best for them. When I read the next round of class evaluations, I did not have a single student complain about annotations.

Balance Power to Ensure Each Partner Has an Equal Voice and Choice

The primary definition of a partnership is a pair of people engaged in the same activity. In the context of a teacher–learner partnership, the shared activity is learning. Traditional teaching models, as stated at the start of this chapter, have a hierarchical structure in which the teacher possesses the power and makes the decisions. However, blended learning models fundamentally shift the power structure in the classroom with the goal of giving students more control over the time, place, pace, and path of their learning.

> Blended learning models fundamentally shift the power structure in the classroom with the goal of giving students more control over the time, place, pace, and path of their learning.

Grade interviews, which we will explore in Chapter 11, are one example of how teachers can ensure that students have a powerful voice in the classroom. My students know that at the end of the grading period, they will have the opportunity to request a grade interview where they can sit down with me and present evidence to support a claim about the grade they think they deserve in the class. Instead of being passive recipients of grades, students have the agency to revise and improve past work, invest time in additional practice, and design their own assignments with the goal of developing their skills to demonstrate growth. If they are not happy with their assessment scores, they have the freedom to make choices that allow them to change their grades. I don't want to be the keeper of the grades. I want progress to be something that students care about and pursue. Giving them the agency to articulate why they believe they deserve a specific grade backed by evidence creates a classroom culture in which students feel they possess power. That can be an incredible motivator.

If the goal of blended learning is to transform "instructional design toward personalized learning with teachers and students harnessing advanced technological tools to accomplish the shift toward personalization by design," then teachers *must* partner with their students (Patrick et al., 2013, p. 9). Without a partnership, it is impossible to personalize learning experiences for a class of 30+ students. Students must have a voice and choice when it comes to what, when, and how they learn. This book will provide concrete strategies and resources to help teachers scale this process of engaging students in regular conversations and reflections about their learning.

Committed to Learning Together

If the teacher–learner partnership is grounded in the shared activity of learning, then both people in the partnership must be committed to learning. When teachers plan a lesson, they ask themselves, "What do I want my students to learn in this lesson?" I think an equally important question for teachers to ask is, "What do I want to learn about my students in this lesson?" To effectively meet the needs of unique learners, teachers must focus on learning about *them* during a lesson. What data—formal or informal—will they collect? This practice of observing students and collecting formative assessment data to drive future lessons is critical in moving toward personalization.

In addition to focusing on learning about the students as they navigate lessons, teachers must be committed to growing in their practice and developing new skills. In my work as a blended learning coach, I find it jarring when I meet a teacher who is unwilling to invest time and energy to learn a new skill or explore a new technology tool. It feels hypocritical. Our job is essentially to develop lifelong learners, and we must model that for students. We must be willing to take risks, experiment, and fail because we ask our students to do these things every day.

If we are willing to fail in front of our students, we send the message that failure is simply part of the learning process. I like to invite students into my failure. If I try a strategy and it doesn't work, or I plan to use a technology tool and hit a bump, I say "Well, that didn't go as planned. Does anyone have an idea for how we can improve this strategy or troubleshoot this technology issue?" I'm amazed by the response from students. They brainstorm with me and offer helpful suggestions. They are genuinely surprised at the start of the year when I admit that something I tried did not go well and ask for their help or feedback. Ultimately, I want them to know that we are in this "learning thing" together! I need them as much as they need me.

I hope this book will inspire teachers to take risks and try new strategies. They may not go smoothly the first time, and that is okay. As educators, we will find our work more rewarding if we treat our classrooms like laboratories where we are constantly experimenting. You may be surprised by how rewarding it is to treat your students as partners in the learning process.

HOW CAN BLENDED LEARNING SUPPORT A TEACHER–LEARNER PARTNERSHIP?

In the traditional teaching model, the teacher assigns work, students complete that work on their own and submit a finished product, and the teacher assesses the finished product. This workflow, as we discuss further in Chapter 3, is exhausting and ineffective. When students work in isolation and teachers assess in isolation, there is a missed opportunity for a *conversation*. Blended learning models allow for a fundamental shift in the way teachers design and facilitate lessons so there is more time and space for teachers to work directly with students to support their individual progress.

In this book, I will focus on four blended learning models that work well in traditional school settings and have become increasingly popular as teachers look for effective ways to blend online and offline learning. Unlike the Flex,

A la Carte, and Enriched Virtual Models, which rely heavily on online learning and online curriculum as the backbone of the course, the Station Rotation, Whole Group Rotation, Flipped Classroom, and Playlist/Individual Rotation Models rely on the teacher's expertise to design and facilitate learning experiences. This is important because I want teachers to understand that their role in the classroom is even more valuable when they use instructional models combined with technology strategically. Instead of standing at the front of the room repeating the same content for multiple classes, they are freed to embrace new roles, like architect of learning experiences and coach helping to support skill development. I would argue those roles are much more rewarding and mentally stimulating than the traditional role of disseminating information.

Figure 2.3 reviews the four models that I will focus on throughout this book. Each role provides students with different degrees of control over their learning. They also function to support a teacher–student partnership when implemented successfully.

FIGURE 2.3 A Quick Review of Blended Learning Models

BLENDED LEARNING MODEL	WHAT DOES IT DO?	HOW DOES IT SUPPORT A PARTNERSHIP MODEL?
The Station Rotation Model	Students rotate through a series of online and offline stations, including a teacher-led station. Ideally, students have opportunities to control the pace and path of their learning, collaborate with peers, and access tasks that are differentiated for learners at different skill levels.	The teacher-led station allows teachers to work with small groups of students tailoring instruction, engaging in conversation, modeling processes, and providing real-time feedback as students work.
The Whole Group Rotation Model **Offline Work** **Online Work** **Conferencing**	The entire class rotates between online and offline work together. Ideally, the online work is personalized for learners at different ability levels or language proficiencies and allows learners to control the pace and path of their learning.	While the class is engaged in the online portions of the lesson, the teacher has time to work with individual students on skill development, conference about progress, or engage in side-by-side assessments.

The Flipped Classroom Model 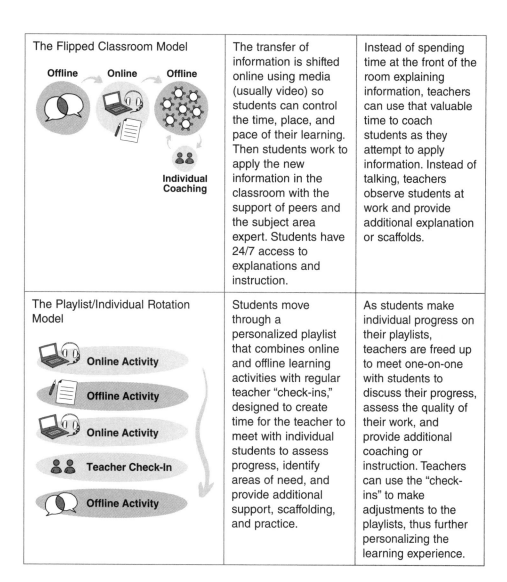	The transfer of information is shifted online using media (usually video) so students can control the time, place, and pace of their learning. Then students work to apply the new information in the classroom with the support of peers and the subject area expert. Students have 24/7 access to explanations and instruction.	Instead of spending time at the front of the room explaining information, teachers can use that valuable time to coach students as they attempt to apply information. Instead of talking, teachers observe students at work and provide additional explanation or scaffolds.
The Playlist/Individual Rotation Model	Students move through a personalized playlist that combines online and offline learning activities with regular teacher "check-ins," designed to create time for the teacher to meet with individual students to assess progress, identify areas of need, and provide additional support, scaffolding, and practice.	As students make individual progress on their playlists, teachers are freed up to meet one-on-one with students to discuss their progress, assess the quality of their work, and provide additional coaching or instruction. Teachers can use the "check-ins" to make adjustments to the playlists, thus further personalizing the learning experience.

When teachers partner with students, they are able to meet individual students where they are in their learning journeys. The conversations, coaching, and support that blossom from a partnership approach to teaching and learning communicates to students that their individual progress is important to the teacher. The teacher becomes a supportive resource and the classroom transforms into a learning lab where everyone is engaged in the process of making progress.

BOOK STUDY QUESTIONS

1. What assumptions about teaching and learning did you have when you entered the teaching profession? Where did these mental models come from? Which assumptions turned out to be inaccurate or detrimental to learning? How has your practice changed over time?

2. Review the partnership principles and identify one principle you feel you do well in your classroom. How is that partnership principle visible in your classroom design and interactions with students?

3. Review the partnership principles and identify one principle you feel you need to invest time in developing. How can you adjust your classroom design or alter your interactions with students to promote that partnership principle?

4. In the description of the partnership principles, did any of the specific examples about how I promote these principles in my classroom stand out to you? If so, which one? How might you adapt this particular strategy or activity for your students?

5. Which of the blended learning models described in Figure 2.3 have you used in your classroom? How did using that model impact your role in the classroom? Did you feel you had more time to work directly with individual or small groups of students? Was it easier to differentiate learning for students at different levels or to personalize learning for individual students?

6. Is there a blended learning model you want to try that you have not used before? Which model would you like to experiment with? How can that model help you to more effectively partner with your students?

7. If the teacher–student relationship was a true partnership, what impact do you think that would have on your engagement and your students' engagement?

CHAPTER 3

Who Is Doing the Work in Your Classroom?

"Don't steal the struggle."

—Angela Watson

The more I work with teachers in a training and coaching capacity, the more convinced I am that teachers are not unwilling to change their teaching practices; they are exhausted. This exhaustion makes it challenging to physically or mentally take on *anything* new. When I present on blended learning models, teachers acknowledge the value of weaving together active, engaged learning online with active, engaged learning offline to give students more agency and control over their learning. However, in the same breath, many tell me they are so overwhelmed with their workloads, large class sizes, and endless district initiatives that they are not sure where they will find the time to try anything new. I get it. I've been that overwhelmed, exhausted, and disillusioned teacher. I remember when teaching felt like treading water. For years, I was trying to stay above the tidal wave of work that threatened to drown me.

LACK OF TIME AND EXHAUSTION ARE BARRIERS TO INNOVATION

I've come to believe that the biggest barriers to innovation are exhaustion and a general lack of time, pure and simple. Teachers don't have any room on their proverbial plates for anything else. And "technology" feels like a big something else. To make room for technology and blended learning, teachers need to assess how they are currently doing their jobs.

- Where are they investing their time and energy?

- Is that investment paying off?

- Are the aspects of their jobs that they invest time into energizing or draining?

- If they could spend *less* time doing one aspect of their jobs, what would it be?

- If they could spend *more* time doing one aspect of their jobs, what would it be?

The biggest barriers to innovation are exhaustion and a general lack of time, pure and simple.

Taking the time to think about and answer these questions honestly is an important first step in shifting our practice from its current state to a more rewarding and energizing future state.

WHO IS DOING THE WORK?

Think about the following tasks related to your job and ask yourself who does these jobs in your classroom?

- ☐ Plans daily lessons and activities

- ☐ Teaches or facilitates the lesson

- ☐ Designs projects

- ☐ Troubleshoots technology hiccups

- ☐ Creates rubrics

- ☐ Provides feedback on student work

- ☐ Assesses student work

- ☐ Communicates with parents about student progress

I bet you answered "I do" to most of these questions. If you are doing all of these tasks, then you are doing the lion's share of the work in your classroom.

That is normal. Teachers enter the profession believing it is their job to do all of these things. It's no wonder most teachers are exhausted.

I believe *students* should be doing the majority of the work in the classroom. Of course, the teacher's role in designing the curriculum and establishing norms is critical, especially at the beginning of the year. But I think teachers, in general, do too much and don't expect their students to do enough.

In the last 5 years, I've made a conscious decision to pass as many of these responsibilities onto my students as possible. My decision was not motivated by laziness or my inability to do these tasks. Instead, I wanted to free myself to invest my finite time and energy into the aspects of my work that are most rewarding and have the biggest impact on student learning, like designing engaging learning experiences, providing real-time feedback, and working one-on-one with students. I also wanted my students to take ownership of their learning. They are incredibly creative, talented human beings, yet they are conditioned to be passive in the classroom. They expect me to do the work. If we do not ask students to do the heavy lifting in the classroom, we are wasting a valuable resource and robbing students of the opportunity to learn both subject specific and life skills. The reality is that the person doing the work in the classroom *is* the person doing the learning.

> The reality is that the person doing the work in the classroom *is* the person doing the learning.

As a believer in constructivist learning theory, I value having students actively engage in designing learning experiences, engaging with their peers to construct knowledge, assessing their work, and reflecting on their learning. Constructivism asserts that individuals "construct their own understanding and knowledge of the world, through experiencing things and reflecting on those experiences" (Bada, 2015, p. 66). To construct their knowledge, they need to be "actively involved in their own process of learning" (Bada, 2015, p. 68). When teachers relinquish their traditional roles as experts and fountains of knowledge, it is easier to invite students into the "process" of learning in the classroom. Shifting the responsibility for work to the students can aid them in developing a much deeper understanding of the content and of themselves as learners.

REFRAME THE WAY YOU THINK ABOUT YOUR WORK

So, how do we shift our approach and release control to students? I was able to make this mental shift with a simple exercise. I realized I had a habit of asking the question, "How can I?" I found myself asking variations of this question all of the time. How can I communicate more with my students' parents? How can I get my students to write more? How can I encourage students to revise their work? How can I make our projects more relevant and engaging? Questions that begin with "How can I?" lead to more work for the teacher, so every time I caught myself asking "How can I?" I would pause and reframe the question, asking "How can my students?" This simple reframing led to a fundamental change in my approach to designing and facilitating lessons that made my job more manageable and rewarding.

For example, when it became evident the first semester that my students needed explicit instruction on academic vocabulary, I instinctively asked, "How can I provide students with more academic vocabulary instruction?" I immediately thought, "I should create academic vocabulary videos and dedicate class time to practicing the words." I caught myself. I paused and reframed the question, "How can *my students* provide more academic vocabulary instruction?"

Instead of creating a vocabulary video for them, students paired up, selected an academic term, recorded a short vocabulary video about their word using Screencastify on their Chromebooks and inserted their videos into a shared Google Slide presentation, so that all of the videos were in one location. That gave students the opportunity to collaborate, think critically, create, and share so that everyone could watch the videos and learn the vocabulary. Students also generated their own practice using Quizlet. They made flashcards and study games to review the words. It was a simple shift that saved me a ton of time, and the result was a more meaningful learning experience for my students.

It's simply not sustainable for one person to do most of the work in the classroom. Not only is it unsustainable, but a classroom where the teacher does the work is also less efficient and less effective. The classroom should be a space where the students, *not* the teacher, are at the center of learning. That can only happen if they are asked to assume responsibility for their learning and be active participants in a learning community.

FLIP THE WORKFLOW IN YOUR CLASSROOM

This shift in mindset seems simple, yet it goes against most teachers' instincts. We place tremendous pressure on ourselves to do it all. In fact, in my work as a blended learning coach, I've found that many teachers are so conditioned to do the work that they feel guilty if they pass tasks onto their students. Other teachers worry about overburdening their students. If we are worried about asking too much of our students, then I would argue that we need to be more judicious about the tasks we require students to complete.

Let's look at two examples, writing and math, that demonstrate how a traditional teacher-led workflow can be reimagined and made into a student-led workflow. By shifting the workflow in both of these examples, the teacher and student work as partners, and I'd argue that students will learn more.

Traditional Teacher-Led Workflow for a Written Assignment

Figure 3.1 depicts a traditional workflow for a writing assignment where the bulk of the work falls on the teacher. First, the teacher assigns some type of written work (an argumentative paragraph, lab analysis, or document-based question), and students complete the writing assignment. The teacher collects stacks of student work (literal or digital), spends hours grading that work, enters the grades into the grade book, and returns the graded work to the students. When students receive their graded work, many simply glance at the grade or points they earned. At this point, there is rarely an incentive for students to do anything with the feedback they received on that work.

This traditional workflow requires substantial time and energy from the teacher, but it requires very little from the students. They simply complete the written work and submit it. The teacher is the person who thinks critically about that work, evaluates the quality, assigns a grade, and documents that grade. It's not surprising that most teachers do not invite students to revise and resubmit work. Teachers don't have the time to do this all twice. But what if we could flip the workflow to place students at the center of this process? How might that impact their learning?

FIGURE 3.1   Teacher-Led Workflow for a Written Assignment

#1 Teacher assigns work.

#2 Teacher collects stacks of student work.

#3 Teacher spends hours grading student work.

#4 Teacher passes back student work, and students glance at the grade. Often there is no incentive for students to do more with that work, and it ends up in the trash.

Student-Led Workflow for a Written Assignment

In a classroom where the *student* does the work, that same assignment could have a dramatically different outcome, as pictured in Figure 3.2. First, the teacher assigns written work, and the students complete it. After they complete their writing assignment, students use a grammar check tool, like Grammarly, to get a report on the mechanics of their writing. They use the grammar report to make the necessary grammatical and spelling corrections. Then the teacher provides an exemplar, or strong example, for students to reference and a rubric. Students evaluate the quality of their written response using the exemplar provided as a model and score themselves using the rubric. Next to each element of the rubric, students briefly explain why they gave themselves a specific score. Finally, students write a short reflection using the questions below to think about what they learned about their skills based on their self-evaluation:

- Which skills were particularly strong?
- What aspects of their work demonstrated growth?
- Which skills are they struggling with?

FIGURE 3.2 Student-Led Workflow for a Written Assignment

#1 Student completes written work.

#2 Student submits written work to Grammarly to receive detailed feedback on the grammar, spelling, and mechanics and makes the necessary edits.

#3 Teacher provides a strong exemplar and a rubric. Student self-asseses his/her own work using the rubric.

#4 Student writes a reflection in a learning log about his/her self-assessment and what it reveals about his/her skills.

- What can they do to continue developing these specific skills?

- What support do they need from the teacher to develop these skills?

I would argue that students are going to learn exponentially more with the student-led approach. Students have to think critically about and evaluate specific skills using the exemplar and rubric provided by the teacher. They also have to think metacognitively about their learning—areas of strength, growth, weakness—to complete the reflection in their ongoing self-assessment document or learning log. This workflow is more sustainable because it is evenly distributed among the members of the class.

Traditional Teacher-Led Workflow for Math Homework

Let's take a look at a math example. Figure 3.3 depicts a traditional workflow for a set of homework problems. The teacher provides students with a set of practice problems to complete for homework. When students return to class, the teacher collects the practice problems from students, grades the problems, enters grades into the grade book, and returns the graded work to students. Similar to the written assignment, there is little incentive for students to do anything with this graded work beyond looking at their score.

FIGURE 3.3 Teacher-Led Workflow for a Set of Math Homework Problems

#1 Teacher assigns math homework.

#2 Teacher collects stacks of student homework.

#3 Teacher spends hours grading student work.

#4 Teacher passes back student work, and students glance at the grade. Often there is no incentive for students to do more with that work, and it ends up in the trash.

Teachers may also struggle to grade this work in time to use that data to design a lesson that provides additional explanation, modeling, or scaffolds to support students who struggled with particular problems.

Student-Led Workflow for Math Homework

If teachers view homework as practice instead of work that needs to be graded and entered into the grade book, they can design a student-led approach that encourages students to evaluate their work and report their scores. This provides teachers with instant data they can use to identify which students are struggling and need additional instruction or support and which students are ready to move on to the next challenge.

The student-led approach begins with the teacher assigning a set of practice problems and students completing those problems. Then the teacher provides an answer key, and students work in pairs to identify the correct and incorrect answers. If they answered a problem incorrectly, they work with their partner to figure out how to solve it for the correct answer. Once they have scored their work and attempted to figure out any of the problems they answered incorrectly, they complete a Google Form reporting their answers.

FIGURE 3.4 Student-Led Workflow for a Set of Math Homework Problems

#1 Student completes a set of math problems for homework.

#2 Teacher gives students an answer key. Students work individually or in pairs to identify incorrect answers and attempt to correct them.

#3 Students complete a Google Form reporting their scores and requesting additional support or instruction as needed.

#4 Instead of collecting and grading homework, the teacher uses the data collected via the Google Form to plan future lessons to meet individual students' needs.

These answers are strictly for the teacher to use to inform his/her lesson and will not count against the students' grades, so there is no need for students to be dishonest in their reporting. Teachers can build a short reflection in the Google Form to encourage students to think metacognitively about their learning and request specific help if there was a problem or problems they want to review individually or as a class.

This student-led workflow has several advantages. First, it shifts the culture around homework. Instead of grading homework, which penalizes students for incorrect answers, it turns homework into an opportunity to learn. Instead of fearing mistakes, incorrect answers become part of the learning process. Second, it requires students to think critically about their work and collaborate with a peer to try to correct their mistakes. Third, it provides teachers with data they can use to quickly identify students who need additional support or instruction.

If teachers rethink their workflows and allow students to do more of the work, the benefits are twofold: teachers won't be so exhausted, and students will learn more. If teachers have more time and energy, I hope they will invest it in experimenting with new instructional models and technology tools. This, in turn, has the potential to make classes more exciting and engaging for students. It's a win-win, but it requires a shift in the way we think about our work. I've found that the more I let go and allow my students to lead the learning, the more rewarding and less exhausting my job is. My students are also more motivated to learn because they play an active role in our classroom.

BOOK STUDY QUESTIONS

1. Where do you invest the most time and energy as a teacher? Is this investment paying off? Why, or why not?

2. If you could spend *less* time doing one aspect of your job, what would it be? Why? If you could spend *more* time doing one aspect of your job, what would it be? Why?

3. Complete an energy assessment. (1) Make a two-column chart, and label one side "energizing" and the other "draining." Then identify each aspect of your job and put it in the corresponding column. For example, do you consider designing lessons energizing or draining? If you find it energizing, list it under the energizing column. (2) Once you've completed this activity with each of your myriad "jobs" as a teacher, reflect on what you have learned about your work based on this activity. How many tasks are in the energizing column versus the draining column?

4. Which tasks from the draining column might be eliminated by putting students in charge of those tasks? Select one task and think about how you could rethink your approach to this task by reframing it using the question, "How can my students . . . ?" Describe how this specific task could be completed by students. How might having students complete this task positively impact them as learners?

5. Put a check mark next to all of the activities below that you currently take responsibility for in your classroom. Once you have identified the tasks you "own" right now, select one and brainstorm ways you can shift ownership to students. How could students complete this task? What scaffolds, support, or instruction would they need to be successful in accomplishing this task? How might taking ownership of this specific task positively impact students as learners?

☐ Plans daily lessons and activities

☐ Teaches or facilitates the lesson

☐ Designs projects

☐ Troubleshoots technology hiccups

☐ Assesses student work

☐ Providing feedback on student work

☐ Communicates with parents about student progress

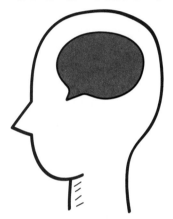

CHAPTER 4

Encouraging Metacognition in Your Classroom

"When students know the state of their own knowledge they can effectively self-direct learning to the unknown."

—Papaleontiou-Louca

THE POWER OF METACOGNITION

Metacognition is the act of thinking about one's thinking. More formally, "metacognition was originally referred to as the knowledge about and the regulation of one's cognitive activities in learning processes" (Veenman, Van Hout-Wolters, & Afflerbach, 2006, p. 3). The ability to think about what we are learning, how we are learning, and what we want to learn in the future are skills that need to be explicitly taught and honed in classrooms. Too often students receive information, learning objectives, instructions, and grades without ever being asked to *think* about their learning or to evaluate the development of their skills. By helping students to develop metacognitive skills, we promote active engagement in the learning process. Students begin to recognize their progress, proactively think of ways to improve, and work through moments of failure.

If teachers are going to shift the workload in the classroom, as described in Chapter 3, students must develop cognitive awareness. Schraw and Dennison (1994) divide metacognitive awareness into two main categories: knowledge of cognition and regulation of cognition. This provides a helpful guide for educators who want to proactively aid students in developing their metacognitive skills. In Figure 4.1, I've divided metacognition into these two main categories and include many of the subcategories that Schraw and Dennison (1994) attribute to each. Figure 4.1 also includes questions designed to get learners thinking about these two aspects of their cognition. It is worth noting that "research indicates that metacognitively aware learners are more strategic and perform better than unaware learners" (p. 460). It makes intuitive sense that students who are used to thinking about *what*, *when*, *how*, and *why* they learn are more likely to be strategic and resilient learners.

> It makes intuitive sense that students who are used to thinking about *what, when, how,* and *why* they learn are more likely to be strategic and resilient learners.

Knowledge and regulation of cognition will help students be more successful when given higher levels of agency and autonomy in the classroom. Students "must assume increasing responsibility for planning and regulating their learning. It is difficult for students to become self-directed when learning is planned and monitored by someone else" (Papaleontiou-Louca, 2003, p. 18). To cultivate these monitoring and regulating skills, students need opportunities to practice planning their learning, evaluating specific strategies, monitoring their progress, and assessing the quality of their work. The good news is that metacognitive skills can be taught, and they improve with practice (Schraw, 1998; Prins, Veenman, & Elshout, 2006).

Teachers can help students develop their metacognitive skills by providing them with opportunities in class to think about their *thinking* in an intentional, consistent, and systematic way. Shifting students from a passive to an active role in the classroom requires that they learn how to evaluate their level of knowledge, understand how they develop specific skills, and know when and why to use specific strategies when faced with a problem. This heightened awareness of their thinking will make it easier for them to set learning goals, reflect on the development of discrete skills, improve their ability to plan and execute complex tasks, make adjustments as they work, and revise their work.

Establishing routines designed to help students develop their metacognitive skills can demystify the learning process and give students the tools they need to be proactive learners. Research indicates that metacognition has a

FIGURE 4.1 Two Parts of Metacognition

METACOGNITION	
KNOWLEDGE OF COGNITION	**REGULATION OF COGNITION**
Declarative Knowledge	*Goal Setting*
What factors positively impact my learning? What conditions help me to learn most effectively?	What are my learning goals? What do I hope to achieve? What specific steps can I take to accomplish these goals?
Procedural Knowledge	*Planning*
What strategies are available to me as a learner? What actions, methods, or procedures have I learned that I can draw from to complete this task? Which strategies have I used in the past that might be helpful in this situation?	How will I tackle this task? What will my plan be for navigating the parts of this task? What will I do first, second, third? How much time will I need to allocate to each step?
Conditional Knowledge	*Comprehension Monitoring*
Which strategy should I select to complete the task at hand? Why is this the best strategy for this specific situation? Have I used this strategy successfully in similar situations?	How am I doing on this task or assignment? What adjustments or modifications can I make to improve my work? Is there something I do not understand? Do I need additional support or resources to complete this task?
	Debugging Strategies
	Is the strategy I am currently using effective? Are there additional or alternative strategies I can try that will help me to improve my performance on this task? What can I do if I get stuck? What resources do I have at my disposal?
	Evaluating
	What did I learn from completing this task? What skills did I develop as a result of working on this task? Is there something I could do to improve the quality of this work? Is there another way I could have approached this task?

Source: Adapted from Shaw and Dennison (1994).

strong positive influence on student learning (Wang, Haertel, & Walberg, 1997, p. 89). Ultimately, students who hone their metacognitive skills will feel more in control of their learning.

Teaching metacognitive skills encourages students to become more aware of their learning, and it can help them shift from passive to active participants in the classroom. If the teacher is the only person thinking critically about learning goals, progress, skill development, and assessment, then the workload is one-sided. Teachers must help students become active agents capable of making key decisions about what they learn and how they learn. This is an important step in forming a meaningful partnership with our students because a partnership demands that both parties are actively engaged in the planning, management, and evaluation of the learning happening in the classroom.

FIVE STRATEGIES DESIGNED TO DEVELOP METACOGNITION IN THE CLASSROOM

When I began prioritizing the development of metacognitive skills in my classroom, students pushed back. They were not used to thinking about their skills and progress. Teachers had always done these tasks for them. At first, students found it uncomfortable, mentally taxing, and time-consuming to think metacognitively about their learning. They had a hard time putting into words why they used specific strategies, articulating what they were struggling with, and evaluating the quality of their work. On several occasions, I heard comments like, "Why do we have to do this?" "Isn't this *your* job?" "This is hard. I don't know what to say." Instead of caving in the face of their frustration and resistance, I reminded myself that a partnership model is grounded in a common purpose, reciprocity, and shared commitment to learning. If I wanted to cultivate a student-centered, student-driven learning environment, students had to get comfortable thinking about their learning.

In this chapter, I review five strategies that I designed to help my students develop metacognitive skills. Ideally, I suggest that teachers dedicate time in class to these tasks, so students view them as central to work happening in the classroom. I know teachers are crunched for time, but we make time for the things we value, and prioritizing metacognition in the classroom will help students develop skills that are necessary if they are going to be our partners in the learning process. Learning must be a shared responsibility between the students and the teacher, but students require support and structure when developing metacognitive skills.

> I know teachers are crunched for time, but we make time for the things we value, and prioritizing metacognition in the classroom will help students develop skills that are necessary if they are going to be our partners in the learning process.

#1 Plan Your Attack

Students are often told exactly how to execute tasks in the classroom. They need opportunities to plan their learning and think about how they want to approach a complex assignment or project. Students must practice thinking about what they are going to do before they do it and planning the necessary steps to accomplish a task. This planning time can help students develop self-regulation skills, which are a critical component of metacognition.

Prior to beginning a multistep task or assignment, teachers can give students the Plan Your Attack document, pictured in Figure 4.2, which prompts them to think about how they intend to complete the parts of the task. The Plan Your Attack document asks students to articulate a goal they have for themselves in relation to the assignment. Their goal might be academic, such as "I want to develop my analytical skills, develop my use of modeling to solve problems, or incorporate more detail into my description." Alternatively, their goal may be personal or related to study habits, such as "I want to manage my time better, avoid getting distracted by my phone, or ask for help when I get confused or cannot figure something out."

Once students have stated a clear goal for the assignment, they must think through and describe the process they plan to use to complete the various steps of the task or assignment. At this stage, students will need to consider the strategies they will use and explain why the strategies they've selected will help them to accomplish their goal.

Finally, students are asked to identify the parts of the task that may be challenging. Instead of being embarrassed or feeling like they are not capable of the work when they struggle, this question helps prime them for the reality that challenges are a natural part of learning. They are encouraged to think about what resources are available to them if they get stuck (e.g., peers, teacher, online resources).

Teachers can collect valuable formative assessment data at the start of a multistep assignment by reviewing the sections where students describe their

FIGURE 4.2 Plan Your Attack Document

PLAN YOUR ATTACK		
	What is your goal for this assignment? What do you want to accomplish?	
	Describe what you plan to do and how you plan to do it. What do you need to do first, second, and third?	
	What strategy or strategies do you plan to use? How will these strategies help you to accomplish your goal?	
	What aspect of this assignment may be challenging for you? If you get stuck, where can you go to get help?	

online resources Resource available to download at **resources.corwin.com/balancewithBL** process and identify the strategies they plan to use. These sections can help teachers to identify potential problems or issues early on in the students' work. Instead of waiting until a finished product is submitted, teachers can skim through the Plan Your Attack documents and get a sense for which students have a solid plan and which students might benefit from an intervention or support.

#2 Learning Log: Guided Reflection

The school day is a blur of activity for students; they are inundated with information, instructions, and assignments. Most students do what they are asked to do, but they probably do not spend time contemplating the value of particular tasks. The learning log is designed to guide students in a detailed reflection of a particular assignment.

After completing an assignment, students are asked to think about the skills they employed as they worked through that assignment. This requires that they reflect on the various parts of the assignment and think about *how* they completed those parts. What specific skills did they use? Did they have to conduct a close reading, analyze or synthesize information, ask questions, collaborate with peers, build a model, describe a process, use context clues to define unfamiliar vocabulary, or conduct research online?

The learning log prompts students to identify the challenges they encountered and how they worked through those moments of struggle. Eventually, students should begin to embrace the reality that facing and overcoming challenges is a natural part of the learning process. This practice is designed to help them develop an awareness of the strategies they can use in the future when they encounter challenges.

Students are asked to articulate something they learned as a result of completing this assignment. Even though most teachers know it is best practice to begin an assignment by explaining the "why" or purpose, it's easy to neglect this when we are tight on time or distracted by the multitude of tasks we juggle on any given day. Unfortunately, if we don't explicitly state the value or purpose of an assignment, students tend to label it "busy work." The learning log reinforces the value of an assignment by prompting the students to identify something they learned as a result of working through the assignment. The goal is to help students understand the value of the work they do in class.

The last two sections of the learning log are invaluable for the teacher. They ask the students to write down any questions they have about the assignment and identify any aspect of the assignment that they want to go over with the teacher. This encourages students to advocate for themselves as learners. Instead of feeling like an assignment is done and they are mentally moving on, students are invited to say, "Actually, I have a question about [fill in the

FIGURE 4.3 Learning Log: Guided Reflection

LEARNING LOG	
Which assignment are you reflecting on?	
What skills did you use to complete this assignment?	
Did you struggle with any aspect of this assignment? If so, what part? What did you do when you found yourself struggling? Did you access a resource that helped you work through the challenging part?	
What did you learn from completing this assignment?	
What did you find interesting or surprising as you worked on this assignment?	
What questions do you have as a result of completing this assignment?	
Is there an aspect of this assignment you would like to revisit with the class or the teacher?	

 Resource available to download at **resources.corwin.com/balancewithBL**

blank] or I still need help with [fill in the blank]." As teachers plow through curriculum, students are not always afforded the luxury of asking for help. The learning log creates an avenue for students to request additional support, clarification, instruction, or practice.

#3 End-of-the-Week Exit Ticket

Exit tickets are a useful strategy for collecting formative assessment data and checking in with students. They can also be used to build a metacognitive routine into class. The end-of-the-week exit ticket, pictured in Figure 4.4, encourages kids to think about what they learned, how they learned it, what questions they have, and how they might teach a concept they learned to a classmate.

End-of-the-week exit tickets encourage a quick, reflective practice while also providing teachers with valuable information about what their kids *think* they are learning. If several students identify a specific concept or skill they are struggling with or have questions about, the teachers can design a station for the following week focused on that specific concept or skill.

FIGURE 4.4 End-of-the-Week Exit Ticket

End of the Week Exit Ticket

* Required

Name *

Your answer

What did you learn this week? Identify at least one concept or skill. *

Your answer

How did you learn it? Describe your process. *

Your answer

What questions do you have about your learning this week? Which concepts are unclear? *

Your answer

What goal do you have for your learning next week? *

Your answer

If you could design an activity to help a classmate to learn the concept or skill you learned this week, what would you have them do? *

Your answer

SUBMIT

Never submit passwords through Google Forms.

Source: Created in Google Forms.

Teachers can use the last question, "If you could design an activity to help a classmate learn the concept or skill you learned this week, what would you have them do?" to identify students who can act as a peer coach for a classmate who is struggling. In my class, I will occasionally ask students who have mastered a particular skill or concept to design and lead a station during a Station Rotation lesson. This way, the students have the opportunity to learn from one another in class. It always surprises me how effective it can be for students to lead the learning. Figure 4.5 shows the lesson template I share

FIGURE 4.5 Student-Designed Station Template

STATION ROTATION: LESSON DESIGN

Your mission is to design an engaging and informative activity for your peers! Below is a sequence you can use to organize your station. Please include detailed directions and any links that your peers will need to complete this lesson. Once you've completed a draft of your station using the template below, share it with me and I'll provide you with feedback.

Time:

Materials needed:

Learning objectives–What do you want your peers to learn/do in this station?

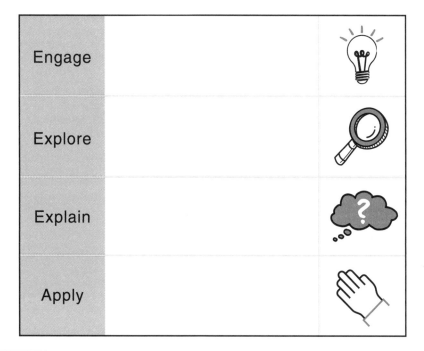

 Resource available to download at **resources.corwin.com/balancewithBL**

with students when I ask them to design a station. Typically, we collaborate on this shared document for 2–3 days before they lead their station. Student-designed stations are a fun way for teachers to co-construct learning experiences with students.

#4 Think-Aloud Video Reflection

Think alouds are a strategy most teachers use to make their thought process visible for students. In essence, a teacher doing a think aloud is providing students with a window into their metacognitive process. I have conducted think alouds when we engage in close reads, analyze a text, or brainstorm for a project, so students can hear the thoughts going through my head as I work. During a think aloud, I verbalize the questions, inferences, moments of confusion, connections, and predictions that come to mind as I work. In Chapter 9, I will describe the benefit of doing think alouds during side-by-side assessments.

Thinking out loud is a versatile strategy that students can also use to surface their thought process. Recording a think aloud can be a powerful strategy that gets students to slow down, think about what they know, describe the decisions they are making, identify the aspects of a task they are struggling with, and reflect on how they might manage those moments of challenge.

Using a video-recording tool, like FlipGrid, to record and share a think aloud has three clear benefits:

- It encourages students to engage in a metacognitive practice.
- It provides the teacher with a valuable insight into their student's thought process.

FIGURE 4.6 Think-Aloud Video Reflections With FlipGrid

 Back to **Learning**

Think-Aloud Video Reflection

Apr 2

In your think-aloud video reflection, please consider the following questions:
–What was the purpose of this assignment?
–What process did you use to complete this assignment?
–Where did you hit bumps and how did you troubleshoot those issues?
–What would you do differently if you were presented with a similar task in the future?
–What did you learn and what skills did you develop as a result of completing this assignment?
–What advice would you give to someone else working on this assignment?

0 Amazing Responses

0 Replies   0 views   0.0h Engagement

Record
Your video will be awesome!

★
Your voice is
awesome!
Share it!

Source: FlipGrid.com.

- It creates a culture of learning because students can watch each other's videos and learn from the thinking and strategies shared by their peers.

Video-recorded think alouds can be used for setting goals at the start of a unit. They can be used at the start of a process or project to get students to think about what they plan to do. For example, instead of writing out responses on the Plan Your Attack, students could record their responses. Think alouds can be used as a "check-in" during a process or project so teachers can gauge how students are doing. It can also be used at the end of a process or project to encourage students to reflect on the work they did, where they succeeded and struggled, and how they might improve moving forward.

#5 Track Your Progress With Ongoing Self-Assessment Documents

Tracking one's progress can help learners to appreciate their growth and identify areas where they need to invest more time and energy to improve. One of my favorite metacognitive routines is the ongoing self-assessment document. It is an ongoing reflection that spans the length of a unit, which for me typically runs 6 weeks.

At the start of each unit, I select 10 target standards/skills that I plan to prioritize during the unit. Identifying my target standards for each unit ensures that I am covering all of the standards I am responsible for over the course of the year and repeat those standards which tend to be more challenging and require more time and practice. I use the template pictured in Figure 4.7, copy and paste the language describing each target standard into the first column of the self-assessment document, and share the document via Google Classroom so every student has a copy.

At the beginning of the unit, students work collaboratively with a group of peers to rewrite the standards in their own words. It is crucial that they understand what the standards are saying if they are going to assess their work in relation to them. Often, this will be an offline station activity in a Station Rotation lesson or an offline collaborative task at the start of a playlist. Once students have rewritten the standards in language that makes sense to them, then they can begin to select pieces of work to evaluate in relation to those standards.

Once or twice a week during a unit, students are given class time to work on their ongoing assessment document. They select a piece of work they have completed that week and do the following:

- State the title of the assignment and include documentation by either linking to online work or inserting a photo of offline work.

- Reference the rubric for the standard and assess their work giving themselves a score from 1 to 4, depending on their level of mastery.

(In Chapter 8, we will review the role of rubrics in assessment and discuss strategies for designing user-friendly rubrics for students).

- Explain their self-assessment score using details from their work and language from the rubric to support their explanation. Students should also reflect on their strengths, as well as the areas that need improvement.

FIGURE 4.7   Ongoing Self-Assessment Document

Ongoing Self-Assessment Document

Unit:

Think about the work you have completed this week. Select a specific piece of work to analyze and reflect on in depth.

- Identify the skill or standard to which this particular piece of work aligns.
- What is the title of the assignment you are assessing? Provide a link to online work or insert a photo of offline work.
- Evaluate your work and give yourself a score based on where you think you are in relation to mastering this skill/standard.

  o Use the rubric for the skill you are assessing to evaluate your level of mastery (1–beginning, 2–developing, 3–proficient, 4–mastery).

- Explain your self-evaluation score.

  o Why did you give yourself a particular score?
  o What details in your work support the self-evaluation score you assigned to this piece?
  o What does this piece show about your strengths as a student?
  o What aspects of this skill or standard are you still working on or struggling with?
  o What specific support would help you continue to develop this skill?

STANDARD/ SKILL	TITLE OF THE ASSIGNMENT AND DOCUMENTATION (LINK OR IMAGE)	SELF- ASSESSMENT SCORE (1–4)	EXPLANATION/ REFLECTION

 Resource available to download at **resources.corwin.com/balancewithBL**

- Ask for additional help, support, or clarification by adding a comment and tagging the teacher by typing @ or + sign in front of their name so they are alerted to the comment. This creates an avenue for students to ask for help and advocate for themselves as learners.

Assessing their work is challenging for most students. It requires that they think about the work they've done, identify a skill evident in that work, evaluate the quality of their work in relation to that skill, justify their score, and reflect on their learning.

At first, many of my students were daunted by this task. They were not confident assessing themselves even with the rubrics as guides. I modeled the process for them and worked through a couple examples together as a class using the think-aloud strategy, and then I gave them time to work in small groups to assess a sample assignment. They were more confident when working with peers, so I dedicated one or two stations each week to the self-assessment form. That way, students would be sitting in groups and could collaborate if they got stuck. I also knew that by building it into our class time, as opposed to sending it home, more students would complete the activity.

As the school year progresses, students begin to realize how valuable their ongoing self-assessment forms were as they prepared for their grade interviews, which I will discuss in depth in Chapter 11. This ongoing self-assessment form makes tracking growth and finding samples of work exponentially easier.

Joanne Weatherby
Science and Physics Teacher
Abbotsford School District, B.C. Canada
@JWeatherby

"Imagine a class where students value their growth in learning and not the grade attached to their work." This is the classroom I wanted to create, but I realized my values did not align with my teaching practice. I dared to imagine and made the conscious decision to change the culture in my classroom from measuring success in terms of grades to honoring the process of learning and measuring individual student growth. The challenge was how to communicate this to the students and help them to track their own progress.

I began by going gradeless. My students would never see a number, only the development of their skills. I taught students how to track the development of their skills and physically graph their progress 2–3 times a semester. Using the graphs, the students were able to identify positive, negative or neutral patterns in their skill

(Continued)

(Continued)

development. Positive progress reflected growth, which increased their confidence and empowered them to continue with this trajectory. Negative progress indicated that a particular skill was challenging for the student. To strengthen and build that skill, students had to listen, read, respond to feedback on their work, which was vital to their growth. Neutral (zero) progress suggested that the student was in a zone of comfort and not progressing. In response to neutral progress, I encouraged students to take risks and try new strategies, so they would continue to grow.

At the end of the semester, the students did not have a final exam but rather an Exit Interview to discuss their progress throughout the class. They discussed their graphs and proved with evidence where they were in terms of all their skill development, and as a team, we came to an agreement on their final mark. There was no averaging of marks from the beginning of the semester. The mark reflected "where they are now in their skill development." We continued the discussion by looking to the future and discussing goals that could help them further succeed in their skill development when starting the next semester.

I imagined, I aligned my values to my practice, I took action in my classroom, redefined success as growth, and valued the process. This is what life-long learning looks like to me and to my students. Can you imagine?

BUILDING A METACOGNITIVE PRACTICE INTO THE CLASSROOM WITH BLENDED LEARNING

Though many teachers believe in the value of metacognition, it can be challenging to carve out time in class to practice and develop these skills. Below are examples of how the five strategies described in this chapter can be integrated into the various blended learning models. Even though I've paired specific strategies and models, these are only examples and by no means the only way to use these strategies. Teachers should feel free to mix and match the strategies with the models.

Teachers who build metacognition into the design of their lessons by encouraging students to plan, monitor, reflect on, and revise their work will have more success partnering with their students and sharing the workload in the classroom. To develop these skills, learners need to take an active role in the classroom partnering with teachers to make key decisions about what, when, and how they learn.

FIGURE 4.8 Infusing Metacognitive Strategies Into Blended Learning Models

BLENDED LEARNING MODEL + METACOGNITIVE STRATEGY	EXPLANATION
The Station Rotation Model + Learning Log 	Teachers can dedicate an online station in a Station Rotation lesson to the practice of reflecting in an online learning log. This encourages students to think about a specific assignment in detail. ● What skills did they use to complete this assignment? ● Did they struggle with any aspect of this assignment? ● What did they learn from completing this assignment? ● What questions do they have as a result of completing this assignment?
The Whole Group Rotation Model + Ongoing Self-Assessment Document 	During the online portion of a Whole Group Rotation, students can update their ongoing assessment form, selecting 1–2 work samples from the week to assess and reflect on. The ongoing self-assessment asks students to ● Select a piece of work ● Align it to a specific standard ● Assess the quality of that work in relation to that skill using a 1–4 scale ● Provide a written explanation for why they gave themselves a specific score This practice encourages students to think critically about their skills and their progress as learners. The more they reflect on the quality of their work, the more likely they are to identify skills that require more practice and development.
The Flipped Classroom Model + End-of-the-Week Exit Ticket 	A teacher can add an end-of-the-week exit ticket to a Flipped Classroom lesson that encourages students to think about their learning that week and complete a series of questions. ● What did they learn? Identify at least one concept or skill. ● How did they learn it? Describe their process. ● What questions do they have? What was unclear? ● What goals do they have for their learning next week? ● If they could design an activity to help a classmate learn the concept or skill they learned this week, what would they have them do? Not only does this activity get students thinking about their work, but it also provides the teacher with valuable data about what students are learning and what is still unclear.

(Continued)

FIGURE 4.8 (Continued)

BLENDED LEARNING MODEL + METACOGNITIVE STRATEGY	EXPLANATION
The Playlist Model + Think-Aloud Video Reflection 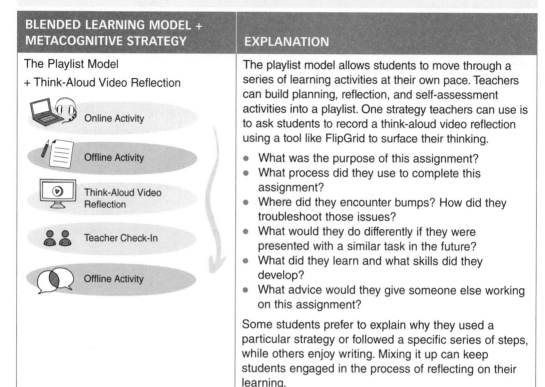	The playlist model allows students to move through a series of learning activities at their own pace. Teachers can build planning, reflection, and self-assessment activities into a playlist. One strategy teachers can use is to ask students to record a think-aloud video reflection using a tool like FlipGrid to surface their thinking. • What was the purpose of this assignment? • What process did they use to complete this assignment? • Where did they encounter bumps? How did they troubleshoot those issues? • What would they do differently if they were presented with a similar task in the future? • What did they learn and what skills did they develop? • What advice would they give someone else working on this assignment? Some students prefer to explain why they used a particular strategy or followed a specific series of steps, while others enjoy writing. Mixing it up can keep students engaged in the process of reflecting on their learning.

BOOK STUDY QUESTIONS

1. How are you currently encouraging students to think metacognitively about their learning? How will encouraging a metacognitive practice support the partnership model presented in Chapter 2?

2. Of the five strategies designed to develop metacognitive skills presented in this chapter, which ones can you imagine using with your students? How might incorporating these specific routines into your classroom impact the culture of learning?

3. How will you respond to students who struggle with or resist these routines? What can you do to support them in developing these metacognitive skills? Are there scaffolds you may need to create or use to help students build confidence in their ability to think about their learning, articulate what they are doing well and what they are struggling with, and/or track their progress as learners?

4. How can you use the responses shared by students as they reflect meta-cognitively on their learning to improve your teaching practice? How might their responses help you to design more personalized learning experiences?

5. Review Figure 4.8 and think about how you might build these meta-cognitive routines in your class using specific blended learning models. Which models do you currently use? How might you integrate a meta-cognitive practice into the models you already use with students? How often would you have students complete a task designed to get them thinking metacognitively?

6. If students push back when asked to engage in metacognitive skill building, how will you articulate the value of these routines? Practice a 90-second elevator speech designed to help students understand the value of developing their ability to think about their thinking and reflect on their learning.

CHAPTER 5

Flip Learning
With Videos

"Video instruction makes me feel like I've been able to clone myself."

—*Kate Gaskill*

A partnership model demands that the teacher and the learner have time to meet regularly in class and conference about their goals, which will be discussed in Chapter 6, or conduct side-by-side assessments or grade interviews, which we will discuss in Chapters 9 and 11. However, teachers who rely exclusively on whole-group, teacher-led instruction may still spend large chunks of class time presenting information at the front of the room. Using video can allow teachers to spend less time talking at students and spend more time working with them.

In training sessions, when I talk about dedicating a class period to conferencing with individual students or conducting side-by-side assessments, I always have a teacher who asks, "What does the rest of the class do while you are meeting with students?" My response is simple, "They are working." This response is often met with looks of incredulity. Many teachers seem convinced that students are not capable of or willing to do their work if the teacher is not providing instruction and monitoring their progress. This perception of students concerns me. I believe the goal of school should be to teach students how to learn on their own. The teacher is there to guide the experience, but the goal must be a gradual release of responsibility for the learning to students. If teachers hold their students' hands through every part of the learning process, I worry that students will not develop the ability to self-regulate, think critically, problem solve, and collaborate productively with their peers.

THE BENEFITS OF USING VIDEOS WITH STUDENTS

For the first 7 years of my teaching career, I spent a significant amount of time at the front of the room explaining directions, providing instruction, and repeating information. Incorporating video in my classroom totally changed my practice. If I am planning to repeat the same information the same way for multiple groups of students, I record that explanation. I want students to have the luxury of controlling the pace at which they consume the information. In real-time whole-group lectures or mini-lessons, students have one chance to access and take notes on the information, and the pacing is dictated by the teacher. That means if a student is absent, tired, or daydreaming, he or she may not get the information he or she needs to be successful. However, if a teacher records that explanation, then students who are absent or kids who are having an off day can access that video content online any time.

To be clear, I view this as a strategy for providing a baseline of information. A single video on a topic will not be enough instruction for the majority of students, but it does provide a foundation on which to build. Once students have watched a video, I can provide small-group instruction and customize the follow-up instruction, scaffolds, and practice for groups of students at different levels.

Video has several benefits over a live explanation.

1. Students control the pace at which they consume video content. They can pause, rewind, or rewatch a video.

2. Students can access the videos anytime online if teachers create playlists on YouTube, share a Google Drive folder with video content, or make videos available on their learning management systems. If a student needs to hear an explanation five times, they can do that without the teacher needing to repeat himself or herself.

3. If a student transfers into a class and has missed important instruction, they can access that instruction online by watching the videos.

4. If parents are attempting to support their students at home, they can also rely on teacher-created or -curated videos to more effectively help their students.

Almost all of my first instruction is via video. Students watch a video, take notes, and engage with the information. Then I provide additional instruction, explanations, examples, models, and scaffolds for students who need more than the video explanation. Despite my enthusiasm for the potential of using videos with students, I know that video is only valuable if teachers design learning experiences that thoughtfully weave video content into the lesson.

Jacquelyn Langdon
6th Grade Language Arts and Social Studies Teacher
Raymond Cree Middle School
Palm Springs Unified School District

Incorporating technology into my instruction has always been a focus of mine. Over the course of my 15 years of teaching, technology has changed significantly, and the impact I have seen on student learning is amazing.

Each year I am faced with the challenge of meeting the needs of diverse learners, not only in style but also ability. Differentiating instruction is a must, providing scaffolds, offering opportunities for enrichment, and challenging students to think on a deeper level. In reflecting, I would often ask myself: How will I accomplish this? What will the other students be doing? Do I really have enough time to work with each student? *Finally, after working with Catlin Tucker, I realized that creating videos was the answer to all of my questions, and I had a solution to my biggest obstacle, time.*

Through video, I provide direct instruction for new content, re-teaching, how-to instructions for projects, and the list continues. Videos give me time—time to conference with students individually, time to reteach in small groups, time to hear my students' discussions and ideas, time to really meet the needs of my students. Additionally, videos give students time—time to learn at their own pace, time to review the instruction, time to pause, think, and process information.

Sure, creating a video takes some time, but with technology and new apps, making a screencast or video is so much easier than it used to be. Plus, the time I gain is so much more valuable than the time it takes to make a video; the benefits definitely outweigh the cost.

VIDEO IS VERSATILE

There are myriad ways an educator can use video with students. There is the classic Flipped Classroom Model, that shifts the transfer of information online so students can control the time, place, and pace of their learning. Then class time can be spent applying that new information in an environment where students have access to a subject area expert and a community of peers with whom they can work. This use of video to provide virtual lectures was made popular by Sal Khan and the Khan Academy. However, there has been pushback against sending videos home with students because teachers worry about their students' access to technology and the Internet outside of class. As a result, many teachers have embraced the "in-class flip," where students watch videos in the classroom as opposed to taking them home and viewing them for homework. Even though students lose control over the time and place when they watch videos in class, they can still control the pace of their learning as they watch videos. I would argue that controlling the pace of learning is probably the biggest benefit of the flipped model. As long as educators build a buffer of time around the video so students can truly control the pace of the video, it is still a valuable way to transfer information in the classroom.

Shifting the videos into the classroom and weaving them into blended learning models alleviates concerns about access to technology and the Internet beyond the classroom, as well as concerns over the amount of homework that many students are being asked to complete after spending seven hours at school. Below are examples of how teachers can use video as part of the Whole Group Rotation, Station Rotation, and Playlist Models to create time and space in the classroom to work directly with students. The goal of using video should be to give students more control over their learning and to free the teacher from the front of the room.

Whole Group Rotation With Video Instruction

The Whole Group Rotation Model is an updated spin on the classic Lab Rotation Model. Originally, the Lab Rotation Model was defined as a blended learning model in which students rotate from offline learning in the classroom to online learning in a computer lab. The increasing number of 1:1 initiatives where every student has a device to use in school and growing access to Chromebook carts has eliminated the need for students to leave their classrooms to work online. Instead, the Whole Group Rotation Model describes an intentional weaving together of offline and online work in the classroom as pictured in Figure 5.1.

When I train teachers on the Whole Group Rotation Model using video content, I suggest they think about planning their lessons in three discrete parts.

1. Begin with an offline activity designed to pique the students' interest, assess their prior knowledge, collect formative assessment

FIGURE 5.1   Planning a Whole Group Rotation With Video

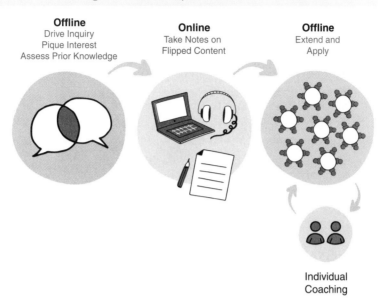

data, or drive inquiry. This pre-video activity is best when it is collaborative and student centered. It functions to get kids thinking about a specific topic and provides context for the video they are going to watch.

2. Ask students to grab a device and put on their headphones to self-pace through the video content. This requires that teachers create a buffer of time around the video so students can control the pace. For example, if the video is 7 minutes, I would allow 14 or 15 minutes for students to make their way through the information and take notes. Some students will get through the video quickly, so having a "next steps" ready for them helps eliminate distractions. Other students will move more slowly through the information and need the entire time to watch and take notes on the video.

3. Once all students have seen the video content, transition them to the "apply" activity. Since they are applying new information, I advocate designing collaborative student-centered activities that encourage students to have conversations and work together. It is often when students are attempting to apply new information that they get stuck or need help. When they do this work in the classroom, they have the benefit of the teacher and a community of peers they can lean on for support.

As students practice applying the new information, the teacher can pull individual or small groups of students for additional explanation, scaffolds, and support.

Station Rotation With Video Instruction

Teachers who do not have enough devices for every student to be online at the same time can build video content into their Station Rotation lessons. Video can be used to frontload information on a topic that will be covered in a subsequent class, or it can be used to introduce information they will be asked to apply in the next station of the rotation. If teachers want students to watch a video in one station and immediately apply it in the next station, they must plan their stations strategically so that students are not asked to practice and apply information before they watch the video. For example, in Figure 5.2, students are watching a video and taking notes in Station 4, and then they are asked to practice and apply that new information in Station 5. That requires that in the first rotation no students begin in Station 5. Instead, there will only be students in Stations 1 through 4, and Station 5 will remain empty on the first rotation. That way no one is being asked to apply the information they have not had access to yet.

In the second rotation, students move from Station 1 to Station 2, Station 2 to Station 3, Station 3 to Station 4, and the students who just finished watching the video will move from Station 4 to Station 5 where they will practice and apply that new information. Station 1 will be empty on the second rotation. This strategy makes it possible to both present new information in a Station Rotation lesson and give students time to apply that new information.

Typically, if I am planning to incorporate an in-class flipped video into a Station Rotation lesson, I do not run a teacher-led station. Instead, I want to be available to coach individual students in Station 5 who are struggling to apply the new information that was presented in the video. Alternatively, I can spend that time conferencing with students about their goals (Chapter 6), conducting side-by-side assessments (Chapter 9), or engaged in grade interviews (Chapter 11). If students are engaged in a dynamic Station Rotation

FIGURE 5.2 Planning a Station Rotation With Video

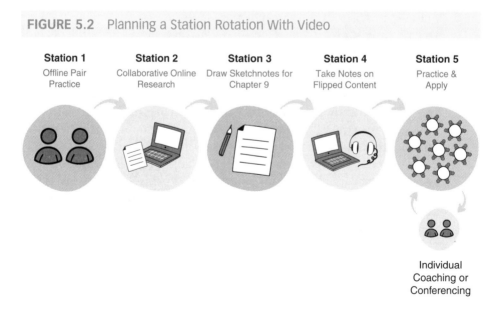

Station 1
Offline Pair
Practice

Station 2
Collaborative Online
Research

Station 3
Draw Sketchnotes for
Chapter 9

Station 4
Take Notes on
Flipped Content

Station 5
Practice &
Apply

Individual
Coaching or
Conferencing

lesson that combines offline and online activities, moves students between individual and shared tasks, and incorporates video, then the teacher can spend time working directly with students.

Playlists With Video Instruction

The Playlist Model, or Individual Rotation Model, has each student work through an individual playlist of activities. Playlists work well for formal writing assignments, projects, and entire units of study. The goal of the Playlist Model is to provide students a higher degree of agency and a more personalized learning experience.

When I design a playlist, I always start with a basic template. I include all of the activities that I believe *most* students will benefit from, and then I customize individual playlists to ensure that students who need additional scaffolding receive it, and those who are ready for next level work are challenged.

My playlists mix the following elements:

- Screencasts
- Offline tactile activities
- Video explanations, instruction, and modeling
- Online quizzes
- Personalized skill practice with adaptive software
- Offline pair practice
- Online exploration and research
- Peer evaluation
- Self-evaluation
- Conferencing
- Side-by-side assessments

The Playlist Model requires significant time on the front end as teachers pull the various parts of the playlist together. However, once a playlist is created, teachers enjoy copious time in class to conference with students, coach individual students, provide personalized support and feedback, and assess student work.

When I design a playlist, as pictured in Figure 5.3, I try to balance online and offline tasks so students are not staring at their computer screens for long stretches of time. There are moments when they have to seek out other students to complete collaborative tasks because I want them interacting with each other. I worry that teachers with unlimited access to technology neglect

FIGURE 5.3 Planning a Playlist With Video

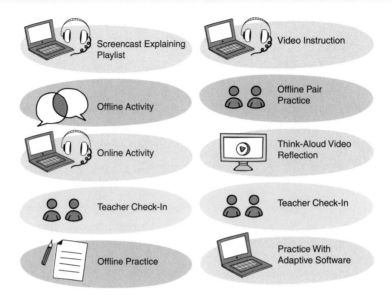

offline learning, which is essential to forming meaningful relationships and developing critical soft skills. Blended learning should strive to achieve a balance between online and offline work in the classroom.

I also build "Teacher Check-Ins" into the playlist. When students hit a "Teacher Check-In," they bring their work to my desk so we can review and discuss their progress. These teacher check-ins are a powerful way for me to connect with individual learners, track their progress, and make sure they have everything they need to be successful. During these conversations, we can discuss strategies and additional practice that will help them to continue to improve and make progress. I use these moments to provide additional instruction, support, and feedback. I also add tasks to a student's playlist if they need more practice or review in a particular area.

Video plays a key role in these playlists because I record an introduction to the playlist, instructional videos, and videos that model a process. Incorporating videos into a playlist means I can use my teacher check-in time to build on video instruction or clarify areas of confusion without having to repeat the same instruction multiple times. Essentially, the video allows me to replicate myself so that students get the explanation and instruction they need when they need it.

ADDRESSING CONCERNS ABOUT USING VIDEO IN SCHOOL

I've met plenty of educators who question the value of video. They raise concerns about the time it takes to produce videos, they point out that it is simply a virtual "sage on the stage," or they worry students don't really learn anything when they watch videos. On all three counts, I disagree.

First, creating a video does not need to be a time-consuming endeavor. In the next section of this chapter, I describe a quick two-step strategy for creating and sharing video content. It is important for teachers to remember that their live instruction is not perfect, so they should not expect their videos to be free from flaws.

Second, the virtual sage-on-the-stage argument is only valid if teachers are recording long lecture-style videos and simply asking students to take notes on the information. I encourage teachers to keep their videos short. A good guideline for video length is to limit the length of their videos to approximately 1 minute for each year their students have been in school. For example, if you are working with first-grade students, I would not record anything over 2 minutes since they have only been in school for 2 years. If you are recording videos for sophomores in high school, you can probably get away with videos that are 11 minutes long. In addition to keeping the videos short, teachers should focus on "flipping and engaging," so students are doing something that encourages them to interact with the new information. Teachers can use a tool like Edpuzzle to wrap a video in a lesson, so that students are asked to respond to questions as they progress through the video. Alternatively, teachers can pair a video with an online discussion prompt that asks students to take a position on an issue or reflect on a topic that was presented in the video. Teachers should not relegate students to passive consumers of information—live or via video. We must engage their higher-order thinking skills when designing flipped lessons.

Finally, the argument that kids don't learn effectively from video does not reflect the habits of young people, who frequently turn to YouTube to learn beyond the classroom. When kids want to learn how to do something at home—apply makeup, play a video game, or build gadgets—many go to YouTube to find a video. This tendency to turn to video for explanations, instructions, and tutorials outside of school makes a compelling case for using video content in school. If students are going to rely on video content to learn, then we can help them to be more effective consumers of video content.

CREATING YOUR OWN VIDEO CONTENT

Teachers often ask, "How do you create your videos?" I follow a simple two-step approach to creating and sharing my videos. First, I create a Google Slide presentation with all of my content. Teachers can use any presentation software, including PowerPoint or Keynote, to create slides, but I like Google Slides because those files live in my Google Drive and do not take up space on my computer.

I have some basic rules that I keep in mind when I am creating my presentations:

- *Less is more.* I keep the word count on my slides low and try to be as clear and concise as possible. I do not want to overwhelm my students with verbiage. Instead, I use bulleted information that I can expand on with my verbal explanation. The more words that a teacher adds to a slide, the longer it will take students to get through the video because a lot of students will try to copy the content word for word.

- *Media is a must.* Media can help to make a concept clear, engage the audience, and help students to remember key concepts. I include photos, graphs, charts, and images in my presentations to help students understand and remember the content.

- *Animations draw attention to key pieces of information.* Adding animation makes it possible to reveal information on cue so students are not jumping ahead to take notes on information I have not explained yet. Instead, I display information as I am talking about it. I also use animation in the slide to underline or box keywords and phrases to draw the students' eyes to specific words or information on the slide.

Once I have my slides ready to go, I record a screencast. Unlike a movie, which records my face, a screencast is a recording of what is viewable on my computer screen and the audio of my voice. So, my students see my presentation projected and hear my voice, but they do not see my face. There are some recording tools, like Screencastify, that allow teachers to record a screencast and display a small image of themselves presenting in the corner of the screen. I find the small video of the teacher presenting distracting as a learner, so I always limit my instructional videos to a screencast with audio.

I use QuickTime on my Mac or Screencastify—a free Chrome Extension—to record my screencasts. The benefit of using Screencastify is that it allows teachers to automatically save video recordings to Google Drive, where they can be shared directly with students. For teachers working with younger students or at schools that block YouTube, saving videos to Google Drive makes it easy to bypass a video hosting site. Instead, teachers can share the video from Google Drive with a link, just like they would share a Google Document.

CURATING VIDEO CONTENT ONLINE

I upload my videos to YouTube and share them with anyone who wants to watch them. At first, the idea of sharing my videos online was daunting. I am not perfect, and my videos are not perfect. I worried that people online would be critical and cruel. To my surprise, the response from students around the world has been incredibly positive. I receive comments on my YouTube channel weekly from students all over the world who have watched and enjoyed my vocabulary and writing videos. It is pretty incredible to live in a time when I can literally teach students I will never meet simply by posting my video content on YouTube.

I realize that some teachers will like the idea of using video with students, but they will not want to create their own videos. Some teachers may not have the equipment they need, the time, or the confidence to create their own videos. That is okay! There is so much high-quality video content available online that teachers can access and use in their classrooms. I would encourage teachers to search YouTube for video content. You may need to sift through videos, but there are some reliably strong video producers posting content on YouTube.

The beauty of using video content to flip learning has very little to do with the videos. The magic of this approach lies in the ability to shift the control and the focus from the teacher to the students. When done well, the flipped learning model—whether integrated into a Whole Group Rotation, Station Rotation, or Playlist—should create time and space for the teacher to provide more personalized support as students work.

BOOK STUDY QUESTIONS

1. How much time on average do you spend in class on direct instruction, modeling, or reviewing directions? What type of content can you imagine recording and making available via video?

2. Do you currently use any video content with students? If so, what types of videos do you use? How do you use them? If not, why haven't you used videos with your students? Are there any obstacles or challenges you face when it comes to using video content with students?

3. What are the potential benefits of using video? Do you have concerns about using video content with your students? How might you mitigate these potential challenges?

4. Which blended learning models do you currently use? What role does video play in those models? How might you expand your use of videos? If you add more video content to your lessons, how might that impact the way you use your time in class with students?

5. Will you create your own videos or curate online videos to use with students? What are the benefits and drawbacks of each approach? If you are going to create your own video content, what process will you use to produce and share them?

6. How can video content help you to actualize the partnership model described in Chapter 2 of this book? How can video help teachers to create more time and space to work directly with students?

CHAPTER 6

Goal Setting

"Goals provide the motivational energy to carry on even when motivation is low."

—Duncan Haughey

When I facilitate training sessions and workshops, I ask teachers to share the most challenging aspects of their jobs. I think it is important to acknowledge the everyday obstacles we face at the start of a training session. It helps to establish the purpose of the training session. My goal is to help teachers leverage blended learning models and technology to mitigate or entirely eliminate the pain points that can make this profession so complex and tough.

Last week at a blended learning workshop, I asked a room full of teachers: What are the most challenging aspects of your job? What factors make it hard to teach and reach all students? I gave them 5 minutes to discuss these questions in small groups, and then asked them to individually submit their top three "pain points" via Mentimeter. Mentimeter turned their individual responses into a word cloud. The words that were repeated by several

FIGURE 6.1 Teacher Challenges Word Cloud

Source: Mentimeter Word Cloud.

teachers appeared larger in the cloud. Figure 6.1 is the word cloud that was created by the group.

This word cloud is fairly typical. Invariably, the words *time*, *engagement*, and *motivation* appear in every cloud that teachers create. It is clear that teachers feel frustrated by a general lack of student motivation and engagement. Teachers cannot understand why students are not motivated to learn. Often this frustration and lack of understanding leave teachers feeling disillusioned.

MOTIVATING UNMOTIVATED STUDENTS

Teachers enter this profession because they are passionate about learning in general and their subjects in particular. That was true for me. I remember my decision to enter the teaching profession was driven by my love of literature. I wanted to spark that same passion for language, reading, and writing in my students. Yet, not everyone is passionate about language and literature. Some students love art, science, or math. Even though I am intrinsically motivated to learn when learning aligns with my passions, I remember studying math in preparation for taking the GRE, and it was *not* enjoyable. I am not mathematically inclined, and I struggled. Yet, I knew I could not apply to a doctoral program without taking the GRE. I was going to have to complete both the English and math sections. So, I dedicated time and energy to the process of re-learning math. Although I was not intrinsically motivated by an innate interest in math, I knew that doing well on the math section of the GRE aligned with my long-term academic goals, so I leaned into the process of studying math concepts I had long forgotten.

I share this example because it's important to acknowledge and respect the fact that not every student who enters our classroom will be intrinsically motivated

FIGURE 6.2 Self-Determination Theory Spectrum

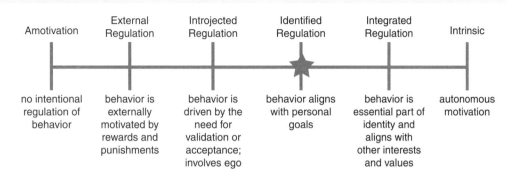

Amotivation	External Regulation	Introjected Regulation	Identified Regulation	Integrated Regulation	Intrinsic
no intentional regulation of behavior	behavior is externally motivated by rewards and punishments	behavior is driven by the need for validation or acceptance; involves ego	behavior aligns with personal goals	behavior is essential part of identity and aligns with other interests and values	autonomous motivation

Source: Adapted from Gagne & Deci, (2005).

by the tasks and assignments we assign. Intrinsic motivation "involves people doing an activity because they find it interesting and derive spontaneous satisfaction from the activity itself" (Gagne & Deci, 2005, p. 331). So, if students are not naturally interested in or motivated by the work teachers assign, what do we do? I believe we must cultivate autonomous extrinsic motivation. Extrinsic motivation involves a separate consequence or reward for completing a task or behaving in a particular way, so "satisfaction comes not from the activity itself but rather from the extrinsic consequence to which the activity leads" (Gagne & Deci, 2005, p. 331). Self-determination theory presents a spectrum of motivation that shifts from controlled to autonomous and includes four different types of extrinsic motivation—external regulation, introjected regulation, identified regulation, and integrated regulation—as pictured in Figure 6.2 (Gagne & Deci, 2005).

I share this spectrum of external motivation from controlled, external regulation, to autonomous, integrated regulation, because it provides insight into how educators can potentially motivate students who are not inherently interested in a particular subject area or assignment. The key is to help them understand how their behaviors and the work they do in our classrooms aligns with their personal and academic goals. This understanding can move students from extrinsic motivation that is controlled, to extrinsic motivation that is autonomous. Helping students to identify and articulate their goals, track their progress toward those goals, and reflect on how the work they are doing is helping them to achieve their goals is one strategy for moving students from amotivation or external regulation down the spectrum toward identified regulation and integrated regulation.

If students have a strategy for setting goals and are given time to monitor and reflect on their goals, they will begin to appreciate how the work they do, though not intrinsically motivating, can help them achieve the goals they care about. I think of it as a connect-the-dots approach to motivation. We, as educators, have to help students to connect the dots and appreciate the value of individual tasks in moving them toward achieving goals that are important to *them*. This is why it is imperative that educators explain the purpose behind the work they ask students to do. Gagne and Deci (2005) point out that there are three key factors that help people to internalize extrinsic motivation

- Explain the *why* or the purpose of the task
- Acknowledge that the task itself may not be interesting
- Provide choice or agency

If teachers considered these three factors each time they asked students to do something, I believe more students would lean into the learning and view the work they do as meaningful. Too often, students are asked to complete work that they believe is simply "busy work" because no one has articulated the value of that work or given them any degree of agency in relation to that work. To create a personalized learning environment "learners must have agency to set their own goals for learning, create a reflective process during their journey to attain those goals, and be flexible enough to take their learning outside the confines of the traditional classroom" (Patrick, Kennedy, & Powell, 2013, p. 4).

GOAL-SETTING STRATEGIES

There are several different ways to approach goal setting with students, but there are four things I recommend every teacher do when asking students to set goals:

1. Provide students with a clear strategy for thinking about and recording their goals.
2. Model what goal setting looks like using a personal example.
3. Provide time in class for students to set, revisit, and revise their goals.
4. Set aside time each grading period to conference with students about their goals.

Provide a Goal-Setting Strategy

Setting goals is a challenging endeavor for students who have never been asked to articulate their goals before. Students need a clear strategy to help them think through the process of setting goals that are both attainable yet challenging. Without a clear strategy, students may flounder and become frustrated, or view the whole exercise as unproductive.

A basic approach to helping students to think about setting goals is to ask them to think about three questions:

- Where do I want to go?
- How will I get there?
- How will I know when I have arrived?

A visual goal-setting map, as pictured in Figure 6.3, may make it more manageable for students to identify specific goals, articulate the steps necessary to achieve those goals, and define what success will look or feel like when they reach their goals. Visual maps or concept maps are frequently used by teachers and are familiar to students, which may make this an easier strategy for introducing goal setting, particularly for younger students. The key is to make goal setting, which for many students feels daunting and a bit abstract, more workable and concrete.

Teachers can also use the popular SMART—specific, measurable, attainable, relevant, and timely—acronym to goal setting. SMART goals guide students

FIGURE 6.3 Visual Map for Goal Setting

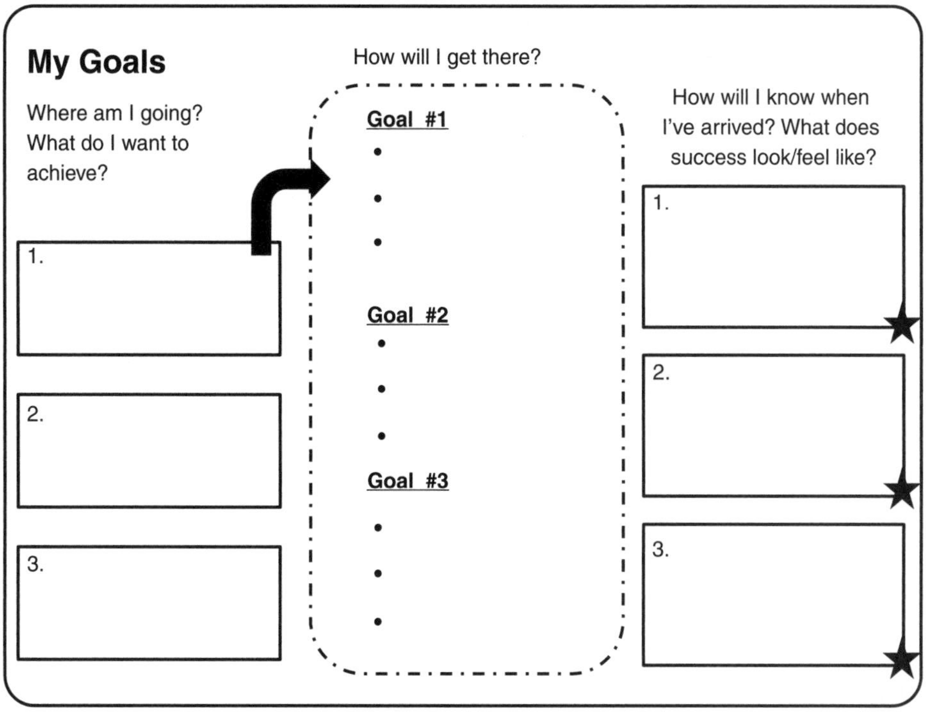

online resources Resource available to download at **resources.corwin.com/balancewithBL** through the process of thinking through their goals in a systematic way. It can help students avoid making sweeping statements or generalizations, such as "I want to do better in this class." A goal that is too general is hard to stay focused on and does not effectively motivate students to take specific action that will move them toward accomplishing that goal. Instead, small, incremental, realistic goals are more likely to motivate students to make decisions that will advance them toward that goal.

If teachers ask students to think through the SMART acronym as they articulate their goals (academic or personal), they are more likely to articulate high-quality goals and avoid generalizations. The SMART Goal-Setting Template pictured in Figure 6.4 asks students to articulate three goals for the current grading period in the left-hand column. I've specified grading period, which for my school is 6 weeks long, because I want the timeframe they are working on this goal to be small enough in scope so that students can experience success within a relatively short period of time. If goals are set for a school year or even a semester, there is not the same urgency to work toward accomplishing that goal. Students need to experience little successes, which is easier to do if they set smaller goals each grading period. As students accomplish their goals, the feelings of accomplishment and pride can inspire them to continue articulating and working toward new goals.

In addition to limiting the scope of time to a grading period, I invite students to set both academic and personal goals. Some students focus exclusively on academics, while others integrate personal goals related to friendships, athletics, or personal habits (often around the use of technology and social media). I believe in the power of goal setting, in general, to motivate behavior. I do not want to limit the scope of the goals my students articulate, but I do ask that at least one goal be academic in nature. Ideally, I would love to have students leave my class and use a goal setting strategy as they move into the world to keep them focused on improving academically, professionally, and personally.

Once students have identified their specific goals, such as "I want to improve my ability to identify whether or not an online source is credible," "I want to develop the details in my writing so my lab reports are more accurate and clear," or "I want to improve my ability to choose strong quotes for my writing," then the SMART Goal-Setting Template walks them through the acronym so they can think through each goal in detail.

First, students must think about their goal through the lens of specificity. Does this goal target a specific area or skill that they can improve in the next 6 weeks? It also asks students to think through the when, where, and how of achieving this particular goal. These questions are designed to ensure that the scope of the goal is narrow and realistic for the window of time that I've designated. Many students will find they need to return to the wording of their goal and revise it based on the answers to these questions.

The second aspect students need to consider is how they would measure success for this goal. What would success look like or feel like for this particular goal? How will they know when they have accomplished this goal? Without defining what success looks or feels like, it will be hard for students to know when they have achieved their goal. Sometimes, the measure of success will be internal, which means the student may feel more capable or confident. Other times, it may be external, where they will rely on teacher feedback or assessment scores as evidence that they have made progress. In that case, it is critical that the teacher know what type of external measure the student is tracking to ensure they provide the student with specific feedback about their growth in relation to this specific skill.

The third aspect of their goal that they must think through is whether or not it is attainable. Is the goal within reach given their access to resources, time, and competing priorities? If not, can they adjust their goal to make it more realistic? What specific support or resources will they need to accomplish this goal? These questions encourage students to think about whether or not they can realistically develop in this area given their resources. It's easy to forget how busy some students are outside of school with sports, hobbies, part-time jobs, and family obligations. There may be times during the school year when they have less free time or are juggling several different responsibilities. It is important for them to evaluate whether or not the goals they are setting are realistic. During grading periods where students have more resources, like time, they may set more ambitious goals compared to grading periods when they have less free time because they are playing a sport, performing in the school play, or working a part-time job.

The fourth aspect of their goal that students must consider is its relevance to their lives. Why do they want to accomplish this particular goal? How does this goal align with their larger, loftier academic or personal goals? How will accomplishing this goal positively impact their lives? These questions are designed to ensure that students connect the dots between smaller goals that may be focused on specific skills they are working to develop in a particular class and larger life goals they value or aspirations they have for their future. This is where it helps them to make the connection between the behaviors and decisions they make in a particular class with their larger life goals. Ideally, this question should help students get closer to "identified regulation," described earlier in this chapter as the alignment of behavior and personal goals.

Finally, students must consider the element of time. When will you accomplish this goal? Do they have a specific date they can put in the calendar? Will they follow a specific timeline or break up the process of achieving their goal into discrete steps or a to-do list? This question encourages them to consider the nuts and bolts of their goal. The more detailed their plan, the more likely they are to take actionable steps over the course of the 6 weeks to accomplish their goal.

FIGURE 6.4 SMART Goal-Setting Template for Students

SMART Goal Setting

What do you hope to achieve this grading period? Set three specific goals for yourself that you want to accomplish in the first grading period. Remember that your goals need to be **s**pecific, **m**easurable, **a**ttainable, **r**elevant, and **t**imely.

Goals	**S**pecific	**M**easurable	**A**ttainable	**R**elevant	**T**imely
What would you like to achieve academically and/or personally this grading period? What specific skills do you want to improve on?	Does this goal target a specific area or skill you can improve in the next 6 weeks? When, where, and how will you achieve each specific goal?	What would success look like for this particular goal? How will you know when you've successfully accomplished this goal?	Is your goal within reach given your access to resources, time, and competing priorities? If not, can you adjust your goal to make it more realistic? What specific support or materials will you need?	Why do you *want* to reach this goal? How does this goal align with your larger academic or personal goals? How will achieving this goal positively impact your life?	When will you accomplish this goal? Do you have a specific date you can put in the calendar? Will you follow a specific timeline or break up the steps? Can you create a checklist with due dates?
1.					
2.					
3.					

online resources

Resource available to download at **resources.corwin.com/balancewithBL**

My personal preference is to share the SMART Goal-Setting Template pictured in Figure 6.4 with students via Google Classroom, as opposed to printing it out. That way, it is easier for me to check in on their progress. I encourage students to tag me in comments attached to the document if they are struggling with a goal or need specific support to continue making progress. This creates an avenue by which students can communicate with me and request help.

Model Goal Setting

Regardless of the goal-setting strategy you use with students, it is beneficial to model the process for them before you ask them to complete it on their own. I remember the first time I asked students to articulate three goals and think through the SMART acronym. Most of the class was stumped. Despite having class time to work through the goal-setting template, most sat squirming without writing anything. I realized they had never been asked to think about or articulate their goals. I decided to walk them through the process of completing the SMART Goal-Setting Template using an example from my own life.

I had just enrolled in Pepperdine University's doctoral program. As a result, I was able to articulate a clear academic goal and walk them through the process of thinking through the specific, measurable, attainable, relevant, and timely nature of that goal. I explained that I was enrolled in a qualitative research class. As part of the course, I was required to attend a public meeting, take qualitative notes, code those notes, and write a formal 20-page paper about what I learned. I identified three specific skills I needed to focus on developing to complete this task since qualitative research required a totally new skill set from me.

My specific goals were to take thorough qualitative notes, properly code those notes, and write a detailed analysis. My timeline was 4 weeks because that was when my paper and notes were due. I highlighted how I would internally measure success based on my feelings of confidence and accomplishment, but I also acknowledged that I would rely on my professor to assess how well I had done on skills such as coding my notes and writing the analysis of those notes.

I acknowledged that the task was attainable, but it would require that I make some sacrifices when it came to the way I allocated my time. As a wife and mother of two with a full-time job, I explained that I would be setting my alarm to wake up at 4 AM each morning for the 3 weeks leading up to the due date for this project. I explained that I work better in the morning, and the window of time between 4 and 6 AM was the only time I would have a quiet space to work in my home without distraction. At hearing that I was planning to wake up that early, most of my students' jaws dropped. There were audible gasps. One student blurted out, "I could never do that."

I responded, "When you want something bad enough, you will be willing to make sacrifices to achieve it." These comments led quite nicely into the conversation about relevance. I explained that I loved learning and had always dreamed of earning my doctorate. This was on my "bucket list" in terms of life achievements, so the early mornings and late nights were worth it. Finally, I described my timeline. I broke down the parts of the tasks that were aligned with each goal and told students that I liked to capture my "due dates" in my Google Calendar and make "to-do" lists using "My Lists" in Gmail.

Provide Time in Class for Students to Set Goals

Once the class had a concrete example, they were off and running. I was impressed by their eagerness to dive into the task once they had seen my example. As they worked, I walked around the room looking over shoulders to see what goals they were identifying and checking in with students who looked stuck.

Setting goals can be a time-consuming endeavor. If teachers send this task home with students, the reality is that many students will not invest the necessary time and energy into the process of thinking through what they care about, how they plan to accomplish specific goals, and what successfully achieving these goals will look or feel like. Teachers often neglect tasks like goal setting because they fall into the "soft skill" category and don't align with a specific content standard or don't appear in a pacing guide. Yet, these are the skills that will likely motivate students to *want* to do the work you assign and arguably make them more successful in life.

> Goal setting will likely motivate them to *want* to do the work you assign and arguably make them more successful in life.

I encourage teachers to use blended learning models to dedicate time and space for goal setting in the classroom. Teachers can create an online or offline station in a Station Rotation lesson that is dedicated to goal setting. Similarly, they can work goal setting into a Whole Group Rotation as a synchronous online task. Then as the students work on their goal-setting visual map or SMART goal-setting template, the teacher can pop in and out of documents, virtually assisting students as they work. Goal setting is also a great way to begin a playlist so that students are thinking through the specific goals they have in relation to the subject of the playlist.

Set Aside Time to Conference With Students About Their Goals

Conferencing with students is the best way to build relationships, develop trust, and stay connected to each student's progress. To build a true partnership with students, we must carve out time to check in with them face-to-face about their progress. Framing these conversations around their goals is an easy way to talk with students about what they are working on, how they are attempting to improve specific skills, and what support they need from us to continue to make progress. The key to a successful conference is to make sure students have the opportunity to have their voices heard during this conversation. The conversation must be a give and take, so students feel it is okay to ask questions and admit that they are struggling or confused.

Tips for a successful conference:

- Articulate a clear purpose for the conference.
- Let students know what they should bring, if anything, to the conference (i.e., goal-setting sheet, work samples, questions).
- Determine a target time for each conference (e.g., 5 minutes).
- Select a location in the room to conference with students so you can monitor the other students, but also have a degree of privacy when discussing student progress.
- Write a list of questions you can use to help students talk metacognitively about their progress and learning.
- Have a strategy in place so you can capture notes during the conversation.

Conferencing with students has several benefits beyond building relationships and giving students a voice in the classroom.

- When teachers conference with students, they can provide them with additional feedback on their progress, which can positively impact their feelings of self-efficacy.
- If students feel like their teachers care enough to meet with them and understand their needs, students are less likely to act out in class causing discipline issues.
- These conversations are a great opportunity to collect formative assessment data that teachers can use to personalize the learning experience for individual students based on their needs.

The trick to successful conferencing is to weave it into your blended lessons. You don't need to put curriculum on hold to conference with every student in a single class period or two consecutive periods. Instead, conferencing can be an ongoing part of your class culture where you are regularly meeting with three or four students a day over 2 weeks to discuss their progress. It should be woven into the fabric of your class, so students feel that you are prioritizing these conversations throughout the year.

BOOK STUDY QUESTIONS

1. How have you attempted to motivate unmotivated students in the past? Have you discovered any strategies that are effective in motivating students who initially seemed uninterested or apathetic?

2. Have you asked students to set goals? If so, what format have you used? Did you give students class time to set their goals? Did you discuss your students' goals with them? If so, how successful was goal setting in motivating your students? How do you feel about allowing students to focus on academic and personal goals?

3. In addition to setting goals, what other strategies might move students down the spectrum from external regulation, where they are only motivated by rewards and punishments, toward identified regulation, where their behavior aligns with their goals, or integrated regulation, where behavior is an essential part of their identity and aligns with their other interests?

4. Do you currently conference with your students? If so, when do you conference with them? What is the purpose of those conferences? Do they take a particular format? If not, what has stopped you from meeting with students to discuss their progress?

5. What do you feel is the value of conferencing for students? How might regular conferencing about student goals impact their motivation, progress, and learning outcomes?

6. What do you feel is the value of conferencing for you as the teacher? How might conferencing regularly with students impact your relationships with them and your overall classroom culture?

7. How does goal setting and conferencing support the partnership model described in Chapter 2?

CHAPTER 7

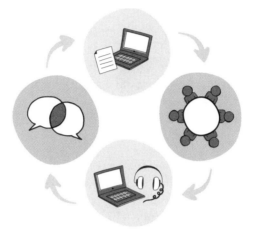

Real-Time Feedback Using the Station Rotation Model

"The key to learning is feedback. It is nearly impossible to learn anything without it."

—Steven D. Levitt

Feedback is necessary to support students as they take what they are learning and apply it. As students work, they need the teacher to provide authentic and actionable feedback that helps them to improve, develop, and hone their skills. According to Hattie and Timperley (2007) "feedback is one of the most powerful influences on learning and achievement" and a critical component in helping students make progress toward their academic goals (p. 81). Feedback can have a significant effect on student learning and achievement when done well. Hattie cautions that feedback is not universally positive and that it varies depending on how the teacher both gives and receives feedback.

Traditional teaching models do not allow teachers the time or flexibility needed to give substantive feedback in the classroom. Instead, teachers prioritize the transfer of information dedicating significant time to explaining information and modeling how to do particular tasks or work through specific problems. Then preparation periods are spent lesson planning, responding to emails, and doing one of the other myriad tasks that consume a teacher's time. That means most feedback happens "after hours" outside of school. Teachers sacrifice countless hours in their evenings and over weekends giving feedback on student work. If the burden of providing feedback falls on teachers when they are at home, it shouldn't be surprising that most teachers don't give a lot of feedback. The feedback they provide tends to be inconsistent and is usually received by students after an assignment has been submitted and is long over in their minds.

This chapter makes the case that feedback should be a regular part of the in-class experience. Shifting feedback into the classroom benefits both students and teachers. Students receiving feedback in real-time can ask questions, request clarification, and immediately act on that feedback. Teachers are more likely to give consistent and timely feedback when it happens in class, *and* it gives them a better sense of where their students are in relation to specific skills.

Teachers can use blended learning models to incorporate real-time feedback into their classrooms and avoid taking that work home. I specifically highlight the Station Rotation Model in this chapter, but it's important to note that teachers can flip their instruction using video or provide feedback as students work on a playlist. There are several blended learning models that create the time and space needed to give students feedback on their work, but the Station Rotation is an excellent fit because the teacher-led station allows the teacher to focus on a small group of students at a time.

In addition, this chapter highlights strategies for using technology to make giving feedback more efficient and presents different approaches to help teachers provide substantive feedback that articulates what students can do to improve their work and develop their skills.

TROUBLESHOOTING CHALLENGES WITH TRADITIONAL APPROACHES TO FEEDBACK

Unfortunately, the time most teachers invest in the feedback process fails to yield dramatic improvements in terms of the quality of student work. There are a few reasons why traditional approaches to providing feedback are ineffective. Feedback is often infrequent, provided after an assignment is submitted, lacks focus and clarity, and does not clearly articulate a path forward for

FIGURE 7.1 Problems With Traditional Approaches to Feedback

PROBLEMS WITH TRADITIONAL APPROACHES TO FEEDBACK	WHY DOESN'T IT WORK?	LET'S FIX IT.
Feedback is infrequent.	Giving students substantive feedback is time consuming, so most teachers do not provide feedback on a regular basis.	Feedback needs to be part of the class. If teachers prioritize feedback as a crucial driver of student progress, it makes sense that class time should be dedicated to it.
Feedback isn't timely.	Most teachers have anywhere from 30 to 150+ students. Even teachers who try to provide feedback in a timely fashion struggle because of their sheer number of students. It is nearly impossible to turn 150 papers around in a day or two.	Instead of collecting work, taking it home, and providing feedback outside of class, teachers must build in opportunities to look at student work as they are working. The scope of feedback will be much narrower, but it will be more frequent and immediately actionable.
Feedback happens in isolation.	Students submit work, teachers take that work home and spend hours providing feedback, then they return that work with notes and comments. In this traditional workflow, there isn't any class time dedicated to ensuring that students understand (or even read) the feedback. Instead, students are left to make sense of the teacher's feedback on their own. If they have questions, they may not feel comfortable approaching their teacher to ask for clarification.	Real-time feedback gives teachers the opportunity to connect with students face-to-face and students have time to act on the feedback they receive. Then if they get stuck, they can ask for help from the teacher or a classmate. In class, students have access to a community of learners on whom they can lean.
Feedback is provided on finished products.	Feedback on a product is not nearly as helpful as feedback during the process. Too often teachers invest massive amounts of time providing detailed feedback on finished products and students are not required to do anything with that feedback.	If students are given feedback while they are working, they can use that information to improve the quality of their work and develop specific skills before they submit a finished product that will be assessed.

(Continued)

FIGURE 7.1 (Continued)

PROBLEMS WITH TRADITIONAL APPROACHES TO FEEDBACK	WHY DOESN'T IT WORK?	LET'S FIX IT.
Feedback that focuses on minutia can be overwhelming.	When teachers collect student work to provide feedback, it is tempting to point out every error. When students receive work back, those corrections can feel overwhelming.	Focused feedback is easier for students to understand, digest, and act on. If teachers select one element to focus on when they give feedback, it helps students focus on improving that specific element and the skill[s] associated with it.
Feedback is one-sided.	Feedback on student work can help students to improve the quality of their work, but it should also provide teachers with insight into their teaching practices. Unfortunately, most teachers make myriad notes, comments, and suggestions on student work, without ever considering how they can use that information to improve their teaching. Even fewer ask their students how they can improve after an assignment or project is complete.	As teachers provide feedback on specific elements of student work, they should track what they are learning about their students (noting trends, gaps, common problems, areas of growth) and use that information to improve their practice. The more teachers examine what student work reveals about their instruction and check-in with students to gather feedback, the more effective they will be at adjusting their instruction, lesson design, and facilitation style to meet the needs of their learners.

the learner. Too often feedback takes the form of quick comments or general statements, instead of specific observations, strategies for improvement, or questions designed to drive deeper thinking.

SPOTLIGHT BLENDED LEARNING MODEL: STATION ROTATION MODEL

One of the biggest challenges facing teachers who want to make feedback more effective is figuring out how to design lessons that allow them the time and space to provide real-time feedback on a daily or weekly basis. Although there are several blended learning models that can help teachers to accomplish this goal, my favorite model for real-time feedback is the Station Rotation Model.

The Station Rotation Model does exactly what the name suggests. There are a series of stations in a classroom and students rotate through them. It is considered a blended learning model because at least one of the stations is an online learning station. Teachers working in a 1:1 environment where every student

FIGURE 7.2   A Station Rotation Lesson With a Real-Time Feedback Station

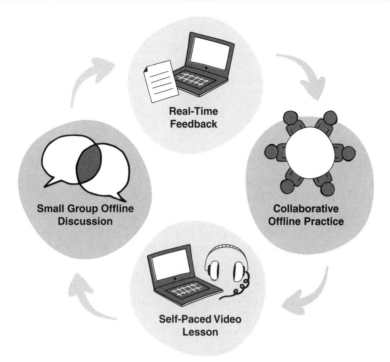

has a device may decide to create multiple online stations; however, I caution teachers *not* to plan every station as an online station. Students need a break from the screen. They also need offline interactions to develop critical soft skills, like the ability to communicate and collaborate with a wide range of people. When I coach teachers, I encourage them to design stations that rotate students between online and offline tasks, as pictured in Figure 7.2.

Giving Feedback in Your Teacher-Led Station

The teacher-led station in a Station Rotation lesson can be used for myriad tasks:

- Targeted instruction
- Modeling
- Reteaching
- Scaffolding
- Question and answer sessions
- Formative assessment
- Real-time feedback

Beyond Direct Instruction

Despite all of the possibilities, most teachers stick to direct instruction because they feel intense pressure to "get through the content." When I enter classrooms as a blended learning coach where the teacher-led station is almost exclusively used for the transfer of information, my goal is to get teachers thinking about the value of their other roles in the classroom (e.g., partner, coach, observer, sounding board).

Crowdsourcing

I understand that in some cases, students need information, and the teacher is the most obvious source of that information. However, students are hyperconnected to information, and they need opportunities to find, evaluate, analyze, and discuss information they find online. Crowdsourcing information on a topic is a simple way to turn the curation of information over to students. Then teachers can circle back to discuss what students learned, highlight important pieces of information, correct misconceptions, and help students connect the dots between the bits of information they've found online. Flipping the script and allowing students to generate the information can be a powerful motivator.

Video Lessons

Teachers can also lean on video content to deliver information and free themselves from the pressure they feel to spend their time with students talking. I tell teachers using the Station Rotation that if they plan to say the exact same thing in the same way for each group they work with, they should just record that explanation, design a flipped lesson, and use their time for something else. Teachers can record screencasts and videos or use already made video content online. There is an enormous amount of video content that teachers can draw on to supplement their instruction or replace real-time instruction entirely. Flipping instruction to allow students to self-pace through information and access explanations any time is covered in more detail in Chapter 5.

As teachers use technology to connect students with information online, they can create time at their teacher-led station to provide feedback on student work. Too often, teachers race through content to keep pace with the curriculum, but it doesn't mean students understand the material or have mastered specific skills. Prioritizing feedback in the classroom creates space for teachers to gauge where students are and what they need from the teacher to continue developing and improving. Real-time feedback is valuable for both teachers and students. Not only does it give students the support they need to continue making progress, but it provides teachers with critical information about their teaching. Where are the gaps in comprehension? What skills are students struggling with?

In his book, *Visible Learning for Teachers: Maximizing Impact on Learning*, John Hattie points out that "feedback aims to reduce the gap between where the student 'is' and where he or she is 'meant to be'—that is, between prior or current achievement and the success criteria" (p. 115). This requires that teachers (a) have a clear idea of where kids currently are and (b) have clearly established what success looks like for a specific task or skill. It is much easier to know where individuals are when the teacher consistently dedicates class time to looking at their work and providing them with feedback. In addition, teachers need to be transparent about what success looks like. What are kids working toward? What does the road from here to there look like in terms of skill development? These are questions we will cover in Chapter 8, which is focused on creating standard-aligned rubrics that clearly state what progress toward mastering specific skills looks like.

TUCKER TIME FEEDBACK STATION

I realize that it is often easier to see a strategy in action before a teacher is comfortable using it, so I want to describe what real-time feedback looks like in my classroom. I teach in a program with a history and a science teacher in what Windsor High School calls a "core." We share the same population of students on "A" days. Our school schedule rotates between A days and B days. Each day, teachers have three classes that are 90 minutes a piece. As the English teacher, I take the lead on any assignments that are anchored in the Common Core Literacy Standards. When our students work on an analytical essay for English, formal lab report for science, or a research paper for history, I am the students' go-to teacher for feedback on their writing. Instead of taking all of this work home to look at and provide comments on student progress, I use blended learning models to provide feedback in class at my teacher-led station, which I affectionately refer to as "Tucker Time."

If students are working on a "process piece" or an assignment that will take them more than a single day to complete, I dedicate my teacher-led station to real-time feedback. For example, when my students write their first argumentative essay, it typically takes 2 weeks from start to finish. That means I will see them 5 days during that 2-week period because of our rotating block schedule. Most days during that 2-week period when they are writing, my teacher-led station is dedicated to providing them with feedback on different aspects of their essay.

I design a series of stations that allow me the time to focus on feedback, because I know that without quality feedback throughout the writing process many will fall behind, some will make easy-to-correct errors, and others will question their abilities and their final essays won't be as strong. In the other stations in the rotation, students engage in a variety of tasks that allow them opportunities to practice skills that have already been introduced or aid them in learning more about the topic we are currently studying, as pictured in Figure 7.3. I try to keep my stations varied so students are not always doing the same thing online or offline. Variety helps keep students engaged.

FIGURE 7.3 Station Ideas

IDEAS FOR OFFLINE STATIONS	IDEAS FOR ONLINE STATIONS
• Read and annotate a chapter in a text • Engage in a small group discussion about a text, topic, or current event • Practice a skill with a partner • Draw sketchnotes for a chapter of reading • Complete a concept map • Use a rubric to evaluate their work • Write a response to a question or topic • Build in a makerspace station • Collaborate with group members on a project (PBL) • Complete a lab, experiment, or STEM challenge • Work on a Plan Your Attack document or learning log as described in Chapter 4 • Create a piece of artwork (e.g., visual metaphor, blackout poetry, artistic flowchart)	• Read and annotate an online article • Watch and engage with an online video lesson • Create a Quizlet review • Test comprehension with an online quiz or review game • Conduct informal research or crowdsource information • Engage in an online discussion • Update their digital notebooks, complete an end-of-the-week exit ticket, or post a reflective blog about their learning • Practice with an online program or adaptive software • Work collaboratively using the Google Suite or Microsoft Office 365 • Use online creation tools to demonstrate learning • Record videos to demonstrate learning or think-alouds about progress

Students do not need me to learn. They need structure and a goal, but they are capable of powerful learning on their own and in groups with their peers. It is important for teachers to value the learning that happens when students work on their own or in collaboration with classmates.

I typically design two types of rotations. I will either design a 1-day four-station rotation, where students spend approximately 22 minutes in each station, or I will design a 2-day six-station rotation where students spend close to 30 minutes in each station. If I am providing feedback on introduction paragraphs and looking specifically at hook strategies and thesis statements, I need less time than if I am providing feedback on the structure and content of a body paragraph. The time I need at my teacher-led station dictates which type of rotation I plan.

When each group of 6–8 students sits down at my teacher-led real-time feedback station, the first thing I do is open each of their Google Documents. I use Google Classroom, so I go into the assignment and open their documents. I always use "Suggesting Mode" when I give students real-time feedback in a Google Document so that my notes are visible in a different color.

Students know in advance what aspect of their work I will be providing feedback on. They should have already completed this section of their work prior to sitting down at my real-time feedback station. For example, if I am

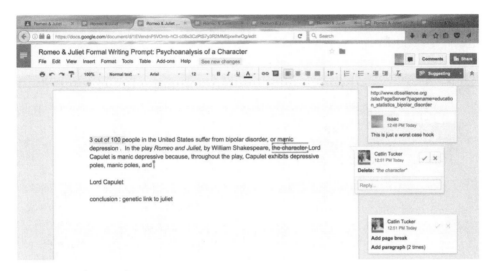

Source: Created in Google Docs.

providing feedback on the topic sentence and evidence in the first body paragraph, then they will have already written this paragraph and will be working on the next paragraph as I provide them with feedback. This way, they have time to write and continue to make progress in class.

My goal in these feedback sessions is to keep my scope narrow. I don't try to correct every single error. Instead, I am more interested in the organization, structure, content, and clarity of their writing. This has been tough. I tend to get distracted by mechanical errors and can spend 10 minutes providing those types of corrections, but in these quick real-time feedback sessions, I don't have 10 minutes to spend providing feedback on each student's work. Instead, I have approximately 3 minutes per paper to provide feedback on a specific aspect of their work. If I don't stay focused, I won't get to every document.

Teachers should identify the specific focus of feedback prior to these sessions and communicate that clearly to students so they come prepared. Technology can also help teachers to provide feedback more efficiently.

Marisa Thompson
@MarisaEThompson
English Teacher

After reading Catlin's post about providing real-time feedback on her students' writing in her Station Rotation lessons and the benefits she and her students experience through this approach, I wanted to immediately try it but was unsure if it would be as successful with a class of 41 students.

I spent two hours planning a four-station rotation. Three stations were dedicated to one aspect of the writing assignment and one station was a conferencing station with me. Students received a slide deck with links to the instructions for each station so they knew exactly what to do when they moved from one station to the next. We explicitly discussed the process and benefits–immediate feedback and zero at-home writing! Students happily agreed to try this new routine and comply with the behavior expectations.

At the fourth station, every student received 3 minutes of specific and useful feedback every day. We also tracked the growth from one day to the next by recording tentative scores for certain skills. I set my smartphone timer to ensure all students got feedback during that station.

The Single-Point Rubric concept made assessments faster and more accurate. I chose four standards-based skills and provided a tentative score for each:

10/10 = I would use this as an example!

8/10 = This is grade level! Well done!

6–7/10 = This needs some work; I can help!

EXCEEDS EXPECTATION (10/10)	GRADE LEVEL SKILL (8/10)	NEEDS IMPROVEMENT (6-7/10)
	Developing an Argument Introduction, Thesis, Body Paragraph Topics, Conclusion	
	Embedded and Purposeful Evidence	
	Depth of Analysis	
	Professionalism Clarity, Organization, Specificity, MLA Format, Grammar, Mechanics	

I record the tentative score for each specific skill, provide a compliment or sugges-tion using ProKeys (see Figure 7.4 for more information on setting up ProKeys), and keep going, all while discussing what I'm seeing with the student. I've organized my pre-formulated feedback by the order the skills appear in an essay, and these comments include hyperlinks to course materials, samples, or even a Google Form, which allows me to collect student work samples for future writing instruction.

They loved knowing I was going to see what they had written, and most felt moti-vated to use the class time. Students said they finally felt they received help on their writing and could see improvement. I also appreciate the chance to sit with individ-ual students and tell them that they were doing well. Sadly, many said it was the first time they had received this type of positive feedback from a teacher.

Students who typically had little work done during previous full process essays came with a completed draft to get feedback. Almost every student returned with improve-ments and specific questions in addition to the writing requirement on Days 2 and 3. Their final products were the best of the year.

Before writing stations, our class spent nearly 3 weeks writing a process essay. I'd spend 40 hours grading their essays at home. Now, students finish their essays and move to a project so I can meet with the entire class for final feedback and scores in the same 3 weeks.

I'm so thankful to have found such an effective and positive approach to writing instruction.

REAL-TIME FEEDBACK TIPS

When I first started blogging about my decision to stop taking grading home and move feedback and assessment into the classroom, I had teachers on Twitter reach out and lament, "I tried running a real-time feedback station, but I only got through three papers in 25 minutes." First, I tell them that it takes practice to get good at giving feedback quickly in a Station Rotation lesson, but I also share with them three key protocols that I use with my students.

1. **Students are not allowed to initiate a conversation with me during our real-time feedback sessions.** If I am trying to give feedback on 6–8 papers or assignments during a 20–25 minute station, I need to be focused on that task. If students stop me and ask questions, it is impossible to ensure every student receives equitable feedback. So, I have set up routines that provide students with an avenue to ask questions or seek additional help without interrupting me or breaking my train of thought.

   a. If I am providing feedback on an online document, they can post a comment at the top of their document asking a question or requesting that I look closely at a particular section of their work.

   b. If I'm providing feedback on offline work, students can capture questions or requests for assistance on a sticky note and put it on their desk as a visual indication that they need help. That way when I reach a stopping spot, I can circle back to that student to address his or her question.

2. **Identify the specific area of focus before a real-time feedback session and communicate that focus clearly to your students.** It's impossible to provide feedback on every aspect of a student's work during a real-time feedback session, so narrowing your focus is key to your success. For example, if I am doing a series of real-time feedback stations on my students' *Lord of the Flies* essays, I might focus on the structure and content of thesis statements on one day. The next day I might provide feedback on the quote introductions, quality of quotes and citations in the first body paragraph.

   If I am providing feedback on a formal lab report, I might give feedback on the students' experimental hypothesis one day and focus on their materials list or the design and procedures the next day. Keeping feedback focused makes it possible for you to give feedback quickly, but it also helps students understand the feedback and act on that feedback more successfully.

3. **Use technology to make your feedback more efficient.** Teachers replicate many of the same comments on multiple papers as they edit student work. Technology can help you save time if you know what tools and strategies to use. (See Figure 7.4 to explore technology tips for giving faster feedback.) In addition, tools like Grammarly can catch mechanical errors for students before you edit their work, so the grammar and spelling errors do not distract you from their content.

TECH CAN MAKE GIVING FEEDBACK EASIER

Prior to a real-time feedback station, it is important to figure out which of the strategies in Figure 7.4 you want to use to save time while you are jumping in and out of documents giving students feedback on their work. I require that students use Grammarly to check their writing before I edit it in my teacher-led station. Teachers can ask students to do that at home the evening before or as a "welcome task" or "bell ringer" activity on the day when they plan to run a real-time feedback station.

I'd suggest teachers set their preferences, create comments in Google Classroom, and/or compile a comment document prior to a real-time feedback station. You want to have all of your comments ready to go prior to sitting down with your first group of students. You can always add to your preferences and comment bank as you work, but you don't want to be creating it from scratch as you look at student work. Most teachers know which comments they frequently use when giving feedback on specific types of assignments. Try to capture those before you sit down with students.

FIGURE 7.4 Faster Feedback Technology Tips

Let Grammarly Deal With Mechanical Errors	It is easy to become distracted by grammar, spelling, and sentence structure errors. As a teacher, it is tempting to spend massive amounts of time editing student writing instead of providing feedback on the structure and content of a student's work. If mechanical errors send you into edit mode instead of feedback mode, ask students to do a grammar check with Grammarly *before* you look at their work in a real-time feedback session. Encourage them to make as many of the suggested Grammarly corrections as possible prior to your feedback station. That way, you can focus on the quality of the content without getting distracted by mechanical errors. This routine also gets students in the habit of checking their writing and correcting their errors. Not only does Grammarly suggest edits, but it explains the errors that the writer is making. Students can learn a lot about themselves and the common mistakes they tend to make by using a tool like Grammarly.

Faster Feedback With Google

Set Your Preferences in Google Documents	Teachers, who tend to leave the same comment or note on multiple papers or assignments can build shortcuts right into their Google Documents.
	Steps:
	1. Log into the Google account you use with students.
	2. Open *any* Google document in that account.
	3. Click "Tools" at the top of the document and select "Preferences."
	4. At the top of the preference box, you will see empty boxes under the words "Replace" and "With." You can enter a code or abbreviation (e.g., awk) under the "Replace" box then put a longer comment that will appear automatically when you enter that code or abbreviation (e.g., Awkward wording. Please rework this sentence for clarity.).
	5. Once you add a shortcut to one document, it will work for all of the documents associated with that Gmail account.
	6. If you are working in "Suggesting mode" (just click the pencil icon in the upper right-hand corner), then all of your in-text comments will appear in another color and create a corresponding comment. This makes them easy for students to see, and if they have a question, they can post a reply to the comment.

(Continued)

FIGURE 7.4 (Continued)

Create Comment Bank in Google Classroom	Google has created a comment bank feature inside of Google Classroom.
	
	Steps:
	1. Log into Google Classroom.
	2. Click on an assignment.
	3. Open a student document, and you'll see the comment bank feature on the right-hand side.
	4. Create your comments.
	5. There are two ways to add comments from the comment bank into a student's document:
	   a. Copy and paste the comments into the document.
	   b. Create a comment, type the hashtag symbol (#), and select the comment you want from the list.
	
	Note: As of the publication of this book, the comment bank requires a few clicks, and setting my preferences is more efficient.

Capture Most Frequently Used Comments on a Google Document	For each type of assignment you provide feedback on, like a lab report, research paper, or analytical response, it's helpful to create a Google Document with your most common comments, questions, links to online resources, and notes for that type of assignment. Then as you provide feedback, you can copy and paste those substantive comments on student work more quickly. Working with a split computer screen positioning the student document on one side and the comment document on the other is extremely helpful if you plan to copy and paste longer comments.
Audio Comments With Kaizena (Google Document Add-On)	Teachers who dislike providing typed feedback or struggle to get through each student's paper in a rotation because typing is cumbersome or they get bogged down in the details may want to try recording audio comments with Kaizena, a Google add-on. Steps: 1. Go to the Chrome Web Store. 2. Search "Kaizena." 3. Click "Add to Chrome." 4. Once you've added Kaizena to your Chrome browser, open the Google Document where you want to leave audio feedback. 5. Click "Add-ons" at the top of the document and select "Kaizena." 6. The Kaizena panel will appear on the right-hand side of the document allowing you to record comments and leave text message style comments. *Note:* In addition to audio comments, Kaizena allows you to identify specific skills that are done well or need improvement. Kaizena has built-in practice opportunities teachers can attach to individual documents to provide personalized practice. Teachers can also create and attach rubrics to documents using Kaizena.

Faster Feedback Working Outside of the Google Environment

ProKeys (Chrome Extension)	ProKeys can help teachers create shortcuts that show up in their work outside of the Google environment. If teachers are working in a learning management environment, like Schoology or Canvas, or are writing a ton of emails, ProKeys can save them time.
	Steps:
	1. Go to the Chrome Web Store.
	2. Search "ProKeys."
	3. Click "Add to Chrome."
	4. Once you've added ProKeys to your Chrome browser, click the green "K" icon.
	5. Create snippets, or shortcuts/codes, (e.g., hk) and type out the comment or email template you want to appear when you type that code (e.g., Hook strategy? For help with your hook strategy, watch this video: bit.ly/essay5hooks).
	6. When you are online typing, simply type the code and hit the hotkey combination (shift+spacebar).

DECIDING ON THE FEEDBACK FORMAT THAT FITS

There are several different ways to give students feedback. In a real-time feedback session, teachers may jump in and out of documents looking at a specific element of the students' work. As students practice new skills, they are bound to make mistakes. Often a quick note or link to an example or video explanation is all students need to correct this type of error. In these cases, teachers may choose to provide more free-form feedback that does not follow a specific formula or layout, while in other cases, they may want to follow a structure for narrative feedback. There isn't one "right" way to provide feedback, but it's helpful to keep Grant Wiggins' advice about feedback in mind when we are sitting down to look at student work. Wiggins (2012) says that feedback should be

- Tangible
- Transparent
- Actionable
- User-friendly
- Timely
- Ongoing
- Consistent

For teachers who want to use a consistent structure for their feedback, both Mark Barnes and John Hattie provide approaches to feedback that may be useful.

Mark Barnes's SE2R Strategy for Providing Students With Narrative Feedback

In his book, *Assessment 3.0: Throw Out Your Grade Book and Inspire Learning,* Mark Barnes (2015) emphasized the value of narrative feedback and developed a four-part approach to providing students with narrative feedback: summarize, explain, redirect, and resubmit. Figure 7.5 is an overview of Barnes's SE2R Strategy with a simple guide to help teachers implement his approach to narrative feedback, with examples that I have added.

FIGURE 7.5 Mark Barnes's SE2R Strategy for Narrative Feedback

Summarize	Begin with a concise summary stating what the student did. This anchors your feedback in context making it clear what your feedback is in response to.	*You [what did they produce specifically?] on the [title of task or assignment].*	You wrote an argumentative paragraph in response to the question about whether or not to add an additional tax to junk food.
Explain	Make observations and avoid opinions when explaining what the student has done. This is the teacher's opportunity to identify the skills that the student has mastered, as well as the skills that are absent or the areas where there is a gap between instruction and application.	*You accurately [insert comment on a skill they demonstrated]. You have also [insert another comment on something they did well]. I did not see [insert a comment about an element that is missing]. Though you have [identify an element that is present], it appears that there isn't [identify an element that is not present]. Did you have [insert a question to get students thinking about the part of their work that is absent or incomplete]?*	You began with a claim that clearly states your position. You have also included a quote from the article to support your claim. I did not see a citation for your quote, and it appears you only have one sentence explaining how the quote supports your claim. Can you develop your explanation of how the information in your quote supports your position over others?
Redirect	Identify the aspect or aspects of the piece that need revision and/or development to guide the students in improving their work and continuing to develop their skills.	*As you revise and edit this draft, please focus on adding [identify the element that needs to be added] and developing [identify the element that needs to be developed].*	As you revise and edit your draft, please focus on adding a citation and developing your analysis of the quote to explain how it supports your position.

Resubmit	Invite students to resubmit their work once they have acted on the "redirect" notes. Teachers should have a clear protocol in place to accepting work that has been edited, revised, and improved. It's helpful to include that in your resubmit statement.	*When you complete your revision, please resubmit this piece [include a specific date if there is one and provide a brief statement about how they should resubmit it and communicate that with you].*	When you complete your revision, please complete the Google Form on our class website to let me know it is ready for me to review it.

Source: Adapted from Barnes, (2015).

For a more detailed explanation, Barnes describes this process in Chapter 3 "SE2R–A Formula for Change" of his book.

Barnes's formula for providing narrative feedback shifts feedback from opinion-based statements to observations with the goal of highlighting what skills have been demonstrated in the student's work, while also identifying any gaps that exist in the content or the application of a specific skill. The "redirect" and "resubmit" effectively guide students to improve their work and reinforce the idea that skill development and learning are a process.

Even though Barnes's SE2R Strategy may feel lengthy for a real-time feedback session within a Station Rotation, teachers can use many of the technology shortcuts featured in Figure 7.4 to provide this type of narrative feedback more quickly. For example, a teacher can go into Google Preferences or ProKeys and create a shortcut using Barnes's acronym "se2r," so that anytime a teacher types that a template, like the one in the shaded box, it appears in the student's document. Then the teacher can replace the dashes with his or her specific notes for that student's work.

SE2R Template

You – on the –.

You accurately –. You have also –. I did not see –. Though you have –, it appears that there isn't –. Did you have –?

As you revise and edit this draft, please focus on adding – and developing –.

When you complete your revision, please resubmit this piece by – and send me a note via –.

John Hattie: Where Am I Going? How Am I Going There? Where to Next?

John Hattie (2012) describes four levels of feedback (task, process, self-regulation, and self) in his book *Visible Learning for Teachers: Maximizing Impact on Learning*. The first two levels (task and process) work well in a real-time feedback station.

Level 1 "Task" is the most basic level of feedback that indicates whether something is right or wrong or if a task has been completed correctly. Hattie points out that Level 1 feedback works well for learners at a novice level. In a real-time feedback station, the teacher may simply be identifying which questions were answered correctly or identifying formatting errors. The goal is to correct errors and identify misconceptions so that the students can fix them.

Level 2 "Process" focuses on the process a student used to complete a task and provides alternative processes and approaches that may be more effective or efficient. Level 2 goes below the surface to drive deeper learning. In a real-time feedback station, the teacher may focus on asking students questions about their work that encourage them to dig deeper, make connections, try another approach, or synthesize information. The goal is to get students thinking more deeply and improving the strategies they are using and the processes they are employing (Hattie, 2012).

In addition to identifying four levels of feedback, Hattie (2012) suggests that teachers "aim to provide feedback relative to the three important questions: 'Where am I going?'; 'How am I going there?'; and 'Where to next?'." To make this three-question approach user-friendly for teachers attempting to provide feedback in a small group format during a Station Rotation lesson, I have developed the following three-part strategy to aid teachers in using these three questions to guide feedback (pictured in Figure 7.6).

Hattie's three questions encourage the teacher to be intentional about articulating the purpose of a task and communicating clearly with students about what it *looks* like to complete that task successfully. Then the process feedback functions to drive the students to think more deeply about their work and provide them with comments and questions that help them to understand where they need to go next as a learner. Allowing students to use feedback to articulate their "what's next" is a powerful way to personalize learning since every student will have a different learning goal moving forward. It also places the responsibility on the learner to think metacognitively about their learning and where they are in their journey toward mastering specific skills. Instead of passively receiving feedback, they must take that feedback and act on it.

If the teacher wants students to immediately revise and reflect on the feedback they received to articulate a where-to-next statement, they must design their Station Rotation lesson with an additional station. I call it an additional

FIGURE 7.6 Using Hattie's Three Important Questions in Feedback Sessions

WHERE AM I GOING?	HOW AM I GOING THERE?	WHERE TO NEXT?
Teacher Task	Teacher Task	Student Task
Before Real-Time Feedback	During Real-Time Feedback	Directly Following Real-Time Feedback

Prior to a real-time feedback session, teachers should: • Identify the target learning goal or skill that is the focus of a particular task/assignment. • Articulate in writing what accomplishing that learning goal successfully looks like and/or design a one-skill rubric that describes what this skill looks like for learners who are (1) beginning, (2) developing, (3) proficient, and (4) have mastered that skill. • Give students this learning goal statement and/or one-skill rubric to provide them with a clear destination or path for developing. *Note:* Read Chapter 8 to learn more about the one-skill rubric.	During real-time feedback, teachers can provide specific process (Level 2) feedback encouraging students to dig deeper, make connections, try another approach, or synthesize information. The goal is to help learners move along the spectrum from beginning to mastery.	Directly following a real-time feedback session, students need time to take the process feedback (notes, comments, questions, suggestions) they received and identify where they need to go next in a declarative statement on their document. This student-generated "where-to-next" statement helps students to take the feedback they received and create their own learning goal or action item to provide them with a clear path forward. These where-to-next statements also provide invaluable feedback for teachers who can use them to personalize instruction to support their students.

Source: Adapted from Hattie, (2012).

station because in each rotation one station will be empty. In the first rotation, as pictured in Figure 7.7, Station 5 is empty because no students can begin at the revise and reflect station. They will need teacher feedback to craft their where-to-next statement.

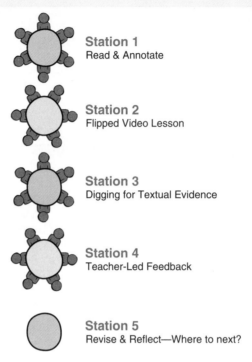

Station 1
Read & Annotate

Station 2
Flipped Video Lesson

Station 3
Digging for Textual Evidence

Station 4
Teacher-Led Feedback

Station 5
Revise & Reflect—Where to next?

Then during the second rotation, the students who were at Station 4 receiving real-time feedback will move to Station 5 where they will revise their work based on the teacher's feedback and write a where-to-next statement. Students can write this where-to-next statement on a comment added to their document, in an ongoing assessment document, or learning log, as mentioned in Chapter 4. During this second rotation, Station 1 will remain empty, as pictured in Figure 7.8.

The beauty of the Station Rotation Model is its flexibility. The total number of stations and the length of time it takes students to rotate through them is totally up to the teacher. Teachers can strategically organize the stations to allow students to take what they learned at one station and apply it at the next. Often the teachers I coach assume that students must rotate through all the stations in a single day, but that's not the case. Multi-day rotations are a great option, especially for teachers on a traditional schedule with short classes. I stress that stations must work for them, the learning objectives, and their students.

In a VrainWaves podcast, Hattie notes that feedback has a large effect size when it comes to impacting student learning. He said, "It isn't about the amount of feedback given. It is about how the feedback is received" (Peters & Kalb, 2018). When Hattie observed classrooms where feedback was given, he realized that the quantity of feedback didn't actually improve the learning.

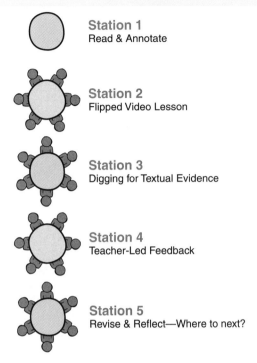

Station 1
Read & Annotate

Station 2
Flipped Video Lesson

Station 3
Digging for Textual Evidence

Station 4
Teacher-Led Feedback

Station 5
Revise & Reflect—Where to next?

More important than the amount of feedback was how it was received by students. He says that a teacher can give the same feedback to two different students, and it may work to help one student progress, but it may not work for the second student. His point is that feedback is received differently by different learners. Instead, it is the "What's next?" question that is critical to helping students take teacher feedback and act on it (Peters & Kalb, 2018).

The goal of all feedback should be to guide students in answering the following questions:

- What am doing well?

- Where are the gaps in my work?

- What areas do I need to spend time and energy developing?

- How can I get closer to mastering these skills?

If teachers have the time and space in class to dedicate to feedback, not only will students have answers to these questions, but teachers will also have a better sense of what they are doing well, where they need to spend more time, and what they can do to support students as they develop. Feedback should be a two-way street. Anytime teachers give students feedback on their work, that feedback also provides the teacher with insight into his or her practice.

BOOK STUDY QUESTIONS

1. How often do you give feedback on student work? What is the biggest challenge you associate with giving feedback?

2. What percentage of your time do you dedicate to providing feedback during the process as opposed to providing feedback on the product? When you provide feedback on a finished product, what are students expected to do with that feedback?

3. What form does your feedback typically take? Do you leave written, typed, or audio comments? What types of technology tools do you currently use to give feedback? Are there any tips in this chapter that you are excited to try?

4. Do you typically give task and product level feedback or process level feedback as described by Hattie? How do you decide what type of feedback is appropriate?

5. Review Barnes's SE2R strategy and Hattie's three questions. How might you adapt and use one or both of these strategies in your feedback sessions? Would you use one strategy for one type of work and another strategy for a different type of work?

6. If you designed a Station Rotation lesson in which your teacher-led station was dedicated to real-time feedback, what other activities might you design for the other stations to keep kids engaged and learning? How can you use technology to free yourself from needing to transfer information or explain things in class?

7. In addition to the tips in this chapter, what other real-time feedback tips or protocols could you put in place to limit interruptions and maintain your focus at the teacher-led station when you are giving students feedback?

CHAPTER 8

Rubrics for Learning

"Rubrics … facilitate student self-assessment, facilitate teacher and peer feedback, and help students envision what to do to improve their work."

—Susan Brookhart and Fei Chen

I vividly remember being a student and receiving work with a letter grade or point value at the top and nothing else. At the time, I accepted my grades, but I did not always understand them. I assumed my teachers possessed a special skill that allowed them to read my work and magically produce an accurate grade.

When I began teaching, I found the strategy of grading without a guide too subjective and unwieldy. The grades I gave in those early years were a holistic reflection of the entire piece. They failed to identify what students were doing well and what they needed to work on. When I began using rubrics to guide my grading, I felt much more comfortable and confident in the grades I was giving to my students. My students also had a better understanding of why they earned the grade they did on a particular assignment.

RUBRICS AS ROADMAPS

Rubrics, if they are descriptive, act as a roadmap for both teachers and students. When teachers make descriptive rubrics available to students at the start of an assignment, task, or project, they serve as a guide to help students produce higher quality products.

Descriptive rubrics have clear criteria and descriptions of what performance looks like for each of those criteria. Brookhart and Chen (2015) distinguish between descriptive rubrics and rating scales. Unlike descriptive rubrics that include both a set of clear criteria and descriptions of performance, a rating scale is composed of criteria and numbers. Although many teachers use rating scales and refer to them as rubrics, there is a distinct difference between the two. The rating scale is easier to create, but much less effective as a tool for students to reference as they work, to assess their own work, or to process and understand the feedback they receive from the teacher.

In my role as a blended learning coach, I have worked with a lot of teachers and seen a range of rubrics. Most of the rubrics I have seen are teacher-created and specific to a particular assignment or task. As a result, the format, content, and quality of these rubrics have varied dramatically. I've seen "rubrics" that look more like a checklist of items that students need to include in their work. These checklists focus on specific elements or particular formatting protocols, but they rarely focus on specific academic standards and skills.

I've seen rubrics that list the criteria or skills that the teacher plans to assess, but no descriptions of what the criteria or skills look like at different levels of mastery. Instead, there is a number scale (often 1–10), and teachers simply circle a number next to the criteria to indicate the quality of work. However, simply circling a number does not help the student to understand what was done well, what aspect of the work needs development or revision, or how to improve.

RUBRIC DESIGN: AVOIDING COMMON MISTAKES

When I work with a teacher who is designing a rubric, I suggest they do the following, as pictured in Figure 8.1:

- Align their criteria with standards
- Limit the number of criteria (four to six is ideal)
- Use a mastery-based scale
- Include clear, student-friendly descriptions of what the criteria looks like at each level of the scale

FIGURE 8.1 Rubric Design

High School Argumentative Writing Rubric ◄————————————————— Title each rubric

Criteria	Beginning 1	Developing 2	Proficient 3	Mastery 4
Clear Claim With Reasons	Claim(s) is unclear. No clear reasons are given.	Claim(s) is clear, but the reasons are unclear, absent, or incomplete.	Claim(s) and reasons are clearly stated.	Claim(s) is clearly stated and the reasons are strong.
Evidence	The central claim is not supported. No evidence provided. *List criteria in left-hand column.*	Attempts to support the central claim and reasons with facts, but the information is unclear, inaccurate, or lacks citations.	Supports the central claim and reasons with facts, necessary details, and citations. *Decide on a grading scale.*	Supports the central claim and reasons with strong facts, thorough details, and accurate citations.
Explanation/ Analysis	Contains little to no explanation or analysis of the information presented.	Attempts to explain and analyze the information, but the explanation is unclear or inaccurate.	Clearly explains and analyzes most of the information presented.	Clearly, concisely, and thoroughly explains and analyzes the information presented.
Conclusion	An abrupt or absent ending. No concluding statement.	Ends with a concluding statement that does not clearly relate to the central claim.	Ends with a concluding statement about the central claim.	Ends with a strong or compelling concluding statement that clearly relates to the central claim.
Organization and Transitions	Little to no attempt at organization.	Attempts to organize ideas, but transitional language is needed.	Organizes ideas in a logical way. Transitional language used.	Strong organization and transitional language used skillfully throughout.
Mechanics (Spelling and Grammar)	Distracting mechanical errors throughout.	Mechanical errors distract at times.	A few errors present, but they do not distract.	Mechanics reflect careful editing.
	Keep descriptions simple and in language students can easily understand.			

Align Your Criteria With Standards

Aligning the criteria a teacher plans to assess with grade-level standards is an easy way to ensure they are assessing skills and not compliance. Too often rubrics are composed of criteria that are focused on whether students completed an assignment the way the teacher asked them to instead of focusing on the actual skills the student should be developing as a result of completing the assignment. If criteria are aligned with specific skills from the standards, rubrics are easier to create and less subjective. Focusing on grade-level standards also functions to highlight for students the importance of developing specific skills in a particular class. Rubrics should make the connection between the task and the skills students are focused on developing crystal clear.

Limit the Number of Criteria

In coaching sessions with teachers, I encourage teachers to limit their criteria. I've seen teachers include 10–15 separate criteria or items on a rubric because they are attempting to assess every part of an assignment. I believe this is counterproductive for a few reasons:

1. The more criteria a teacher includes, the longer it will take to assess student work.

2. A rubric with too many items is less helpful as a guide when students are working on an assignment.

3. Too many criteria can make the process of using the rubric for self-assessment more challenging and cumbersome for students.

4. When students receive a rubric with feedback on too many items, it is overwhelming and hard to act on all of that feedback.

Use a Mastery-Based Scale

Descriptive rubrics articulate at each level what the criteria look like, so it is important to choose a scale that is manageable. Many teachers still use the 10-point scale as it is easier to convert to a 100-point score, but I suggest a 4-point mastery-based scale. My decision to embrace a 4-point scale has to do with simplicity more than anything else. I use the following scale: 1 = beginning; 2 = developing; 3 = proficient; 4 = mastery. I want my rubrics to send a clear message to my students that the goal of our class is to move toward mastering specific skills.

Include Clear, Student-Friendly Descriptions

Articulating what skills look like at each level of mastery is the most challenging aspect of creating a rubric, which is why some teachers simply use numbers and do not include descriptions. Unfortunately, a rubric that does not describe what the skill looks like at each level will not be a useful tool for students. Students need to understand what the difference is between a skill that receives a score of a 2 versus a score of 3. By including clear descriptions

FIGURE 8.2 Rubric Template

CRITERIA	BEGINNING 1	DEVELOPING 2	PROFICIENT 3	MASTERY 4

 Resource available to download at **resources.corwin.com/balancewithBL**

written in student-friendly language, students will know exactly what the teacher saw while assessing their work and what they need to do to improve that specific skill and move to the next level of mastery.

The rubric template pictured in Figure 8.2 can be copied and modified for any teacher who wants to design their rubrics using a consistent style and structure.

USING RUBRICS TO FURTHER STUDENT LEARNING

In addition to the design flaws that exist in a lot of rubrics, many students never see the rubric the teacher is using to assess their skills until they receive their graded work back. This is a missed opportunity.

Rubrics can

- Guide students as they work
- Encourage self-assessment
- Support reflection and metacognition

Rubrics Can Guide Students as They Work

Rubrics can make the expectations for a particular assignment clear and provide students with support as they work. Panadero, Tapia, and Huertas (2012) argue that the teacher's "assessment criteria must be clear to the student from the beginning of the learning processes so that the students can have clear expectations about what their goals are and plan accordingly" (p. 807). Ideally, a rubric should be provided as soon as the teacher assigns work that he or she intends to assess. That way, students know exactly how that work will be assessed and what they need to do to work toward mastery. If students have a clear idea of how their work will be evaluated and which skills will be assessed, they can focus on developing those specific skills. This creates more transparency around the grading process, which is often opaque from the student perspective.

Rubrics Can Encourage Self-Assessment

Rubrics are not simply teaching tools that make grading easier. Rubrics "are self-assessment tools with three characteristics: a list of criteria for assessing the important goals of the task, a scale for grading the different levels of achievement and a description for each qualitative level" (Panadero et al., 2012, p. 807). They can be used to engage students in the process of evaluating the quality of their work prior to a final assessment. When I am coaching teachers, I suggest that they have students complete a self-assessment of their work using the rubric that the teacher intends to use *prior* to the side-by-side assessments, which are described in Chapter 9.

It's valuable for students to assess the quality of their work using the same rubric that the teacher will be using. Research has shown that rubrics have a positive impact on students' ability to self-regulate and on their feelings of self-efficacy (Panadero et al., 2012). Looking at their work through the lens of specific skills can help students to identify areas of strength and weakness in time to request support or make edits prior to submitting a final draft.

When students complete a self-assessment using a rubric, I ask that they give themselves a score for each skill included on the rubric and write a justification for the score they gave themselves. This motivates them to think critically about their work, read through the descriptions of the criteria at each level of mastery, and then explain their choice using details from their work to support their assessment scores. Requiring students to self-assess also reinforces the partnership model because both the student and teacher are looking critically at the quality of work that the student is producing.

To make self-assessment easy for students, I simply take my existing rubric, make a copy of it, and add an additional "score" column as pictured in Figure 8.3. Then as students assess their own work, they circle the language that they believe best aligns with the quality of their work for each skill. Then

FIGURE 8.3 Rubric With Self-assessment Column

Name:

Date:

Class:

High School Argumentative Writing Rubric

Add an additional column for the student's self-assessment score and explanation

CRITERIA	BEGINNING 1	DEVELOPING 2	PROFICIENT 3	MASTERY 4	SCORE WHY DID YOU GIVE YOURSELF THIS SCORE?
CLEAR CLAIM WITH REASONS	Claim(s) is unclear. No clear reasons are given.	Claim(s) is clear, but the reasons are unclear, absent, or incomplete.	Claim(s) and reasons are clearly stated.	Claim(s) is clearly stated and the reasons are strong.	
EVIDENCE	The central claim is not supported. No evidence provided.	Attempts to support the central claim and reasons with facts, but the information is unclear, inaccurate, or lacks citations.	Supports the central claim and reasons with facts, necessary details, and citations.	Supports the central claim and reasons with strong facts, thorough details, and accurate citations.	
EXPLANATION/ ANALYSIS	Contains little to no explanation or analysis of the information presented.	Attempts to explain and analyze the information, but the explanation is unclear or inaccurate.	Clearly explains and analyzes most of the information presented.	Clearly, concisely, and thoroughly explains and analyzes the information presented.	
CONCLUSION	An abrupt or absent ending. No concluding statement.	Ends with a concluding statement that does not clearly relate to the central claim.	Ends with a concluding statement about the central claim.	Ends with a strong or compelling concluding statement that clearly relates to the central claim.	
ORGANIZATION AND TRANSITIONS	Little to no attempt at organization.	Attempts to organize ideas, but transitional language is needed.	Organizes ideas in a logical way. Transitional language used.	Strong organization and transitional language used skillfully throughout.	
MECHANICS (SPELLING AND GRAMMAR)	Distracting mechanical errors throughout.	Mechanical errors distract at times.	A few errors present, but they do not distract.	Mechanics reflect careful editing.	

they write a short justification for the score they gave themselves. I ask them to point to specific details in their work to support their scores.

These self-assessment scores can be useful reference points when having conversations with students about their progress. If students have given themselves a significantly higher or lower score than I would have on a specific skill, this may signal that the student does not understand the expectation, is being too critical of his or her work, or needs additional support. This creates transparency around student progress and presents an opportunity for a conversation about what the student needs from me in terms of instruction, support, feedback, or additional practice to continue making progress toward mastery of specific skills.

I ask that students bring the rubric with their self-assessment scores to our side-by-side assessments, which we will discuss in the next chapter. As I assess each student's scores on my rubric, I compare our two sets of scores. Normally, our scores are similar, but there are moments when the scores are so disparate that we need to have a conversation about why they scored their work the way they did.

Ely Jauregui
English I CP/ AVID 11
Rancho Mirage High School

My AVID students wrote a college essay for their first-semester final. I took 73 essays home to grade. I was dreading it. I stumbled onto Catlin's blog that asked the question, "Who is doing the work in the classroom? Who is really learning?" This caused me to stop and reflect on my practice. In the post, she suggested that students self-assess their work using a rubric. Instead of grading the 73 essays, I took them back to school and passed them back to the students.

AVID already had a CSU rubric for college essays so I made a copy for each student. First, we talked about the rubric to ensure they understood the criteria. Then I asked them to highlight specific aspects of their essays and instructed them to score their essays using the rubrics. In addition to scoring the various elements of their paper using the CSU rubric, I asked them to write down two elements of their writing that they felt they needed to focus on improving.

Not only did having students assess their own essays save me a ton of time, but it required that they think metacognitively about their writing and reflect on their skills. This exercise helped them to realize that writing is a process. The practice of regular self-assessment empowers students to identify what needs improvement and proactively develop their skills. I want my students to understand that learning is so much more than a grade at the top of the paper.

Rubrics Support Reflection and Metacognition

Rubrics capture a student's skill set at a particular moment in time. This can be a useful tool for students who are reflecting on their growth or identifying areas they want to focus on improving. The rubric should support the process of completing a learning log or updating an ongoing assessment document, as discussed in Chapter 4. The rubric should give students a clear sense of where they are and where they want to go in terms of their progress.

YOU DON'T NEED TO ASSESS EVERY ASPECT OF EVERY ASSIGNMENT

Teachers place immense pressure on themselves to grade *everything*. However, our desire to be thorough as we assess student work can overwhelm students. A rubric might have four to six criteria on it, but that does not mean that the teacher has to assess every criterion every time. For example, at the beginning of the school year when students complete their first piece of argumentative writing, I use the rubric pictured in Figure 8.1, but I do *not* assess all six criteria. Instead, I narrow the focus of that assessment to three criteria, such as claim, evidence, and organization, since those are the aspects of argumentative writing that I tend to emphasize at the start of the year. By focusing on skills we have spent time developing, I avoid penalizing students for their mechanics or the depth of their analysis when we have not had time to drill down into those skills. Later in the year, I might shift my focus to assess evidence, analysis, and mechanics because we have spent more time on those skills.

Teachers often ask, "Do students get upset that you don't grade everything?" No. I think most students are relieved that I have kept my focus narrow. In fact, by limiting my assessment to three criteria, I avoid inundating students with more information than they can realistically take in and act upon. If a student receives a rubric with 10 criteria that have each been assessed, he or she is unlikely to read through the description that the teacher has circled for each skill. Instead, if the teachers narrows the scope of the assessment to three criteria, even if the actual rubric has more criteria than that, it is more manageable for students to make sense of what they did well and what they need to work on in the future.

Additionally, rubrics with too many criteria make conducting side-by-side assessments (Chapter 9) more challenging and time-consuming. If we are grading student work with students sitting next to us, it is helpful to limit the scope of the assessment to ensure this practice is sustainable. The longer it takes to grade student work, the less invested students are in their final scores and the less likely they are to attempt revisions.

If teachers are using a multi-skill rubric and assessing a few separate criteria, I encourage them to enter each skill into the grade book separately. Too often teachers dump a collection of points into the grade book for an assignment even though they have evaluated individual skills. Entering 82/100 into the grade book for a formal piece of writing or a project does not clearly communicate to the student or their parents exactly what was done well and what was missing or underdeveloped. Instead, if each skill is entered separately into the grade book, it creates clarity about the quality of the students' work. For example, a history teacher who is assessing an infographic (or visual representation of research) might choose to assess the quality of research, integration of quantitative information and use of media to communicate data, and clarity of the central theme, claim, or message in the infographic.

Infographic Project–Quality of Research	3/4
Infographic Project–Integration of Quantitative Information & Use of Media	2/4
Infographic Project–Clarity of Central Theme, Claim, or Message	1.5/4

This clearly communicates how students are doing in relation to specific skills and makes tracking progress toward mastery easier. It also means that teachers who are under pressure from their administrations to enter a specific number of items in the grade book per week or grading period can be more judicious about what they grade, while still having a respectable number of assessment scores in the grade book.

SINGLE SKILL RUBRIC: LESS IS MORE

The single skill rubric is my favorite new approach to using rubrics. A single skill rubric is a rubric that has a single criterion. For example, I made the single skill rubric that appears in Figure 8.4 to assess RL.1, which is the first reading literature standard in the Common Core. I took the standard which reads "cite several pieces of textual evidence to support analysis of what the text says explicitly as well as inferences drawn from the text." Then I spent time thinking about what that skill would look like in the four stages of mastery–beginning, developing, proficient, and mastery. I wrote descriptions for each level. Then when I want to assess this particular skill, I simply use this one skill rubric.

The one skill rubric makes assessing student work less daunting because teachers do not feel pressure to assess more than a single skill at a time. This makes it more manageable to move the assessment process into the classroom. Instead of treating every assessment like a time-consuming event, which is stressful for

FIGURE 8.4   Single Skill Rubric for Reading Literature 9–10.1

Skill/Standard: RL.1–Cite several pieces of textual evidence to support analysis of what the text says explicitly as well as inferences drawn from the text.

1 BEGINNING	2 DEVELOPING	3 PROFICIENT	4 MASTERY
Cites textual evidence (quotes from the text) but the textual evidence used does not clearly support or relate to the analysis of what the text says explicitly.	Cites textual evidence (quotes from the text) that supports some of the analysis of what the text says explicity.	Cites strong textual evidence (quotes from the text) that supports the analysis of what the text says explicitly as well as some inferences drawn from the text.	Cites strong and thorough textual evidence (quotes from the text) that clearly support analysis of what the text says explicitly and implicity.

both teachers and students, teachers can scale down the scope of the assessments administering more frequent, smaller scale assessments.

For example, the ability to engage in a small-group discussion is a speaking and listening skill that my students are expected to develop. If I am using a single skill rubric that targets student participation in a small-group discussion, as pictured in Figure 8.5, it does not take long to observe a group and assess each student's discussion skills. I simply circle the language on the single skill discussion rubric that captures the skills I am seeing.

If I am using the single skill rubric as a formative assessment tool, I give students their slip of paper with their score, so they know what I am seeing when I watch them engage in a discussion. It's important for students to receive this type of feedback prior to a summative assessment that will be recorded in the grade book. Once we have spent time practicing this skill, then I will use the exact same rubric and give students a summative assessment score.

Two years ago, I decided to create a single-skill rubric for each of the standards my students were responsible for in our English class. I posted them along with my multi-skill rubrics on my class website at the beginning of the year, so students and parents had access to them. Anytime I assigned something that I planned to assess, I told the students exactly which single or multi-skill rubric I planned to use to assess their work. That way, there was no opacity around what or how I was assessing. Figure 8.6 is a template that teachers can copy and use to create their own single-skill rubrics.

In addition to making assessment more manageable, I've had several students tell me that they like the simplicity of the single skill rubric. One student remarked that receiving an assessment score on a single skill was "motivating" because it made it clear exactly what they needed to work on in relation to that skill. Another student said the single skill rubric made assessments "less scary" because if they didn't do well, it was just one skill, and it didn't have a huge negative impact on his grade.

FIGURE 8.5 Single Skill Rubric for Speaking & Listening 9–10.1 A-D

Skill/Standard: SL.9–10.1 A-D

Initiate and participate effectively in a range of collaborative discussions (one-on-one, in groups, and teacher-led) with diverse partners on grades 9–10 topics, texts, and issues, building on others' ideas and expressing their own clearly and persuasively.

1 BEGINNING	2 DEVELOPING	3 PROFICIENT	4 MASTERY
Little to no participation in discussion. Does not come to discussions prepared and fails to support statements with evidence from texts. Few attempts to ask questions or build ideas shared.	Limited participation in discussions. Does not consistently come to discussions prepared. Limited attempts to support statements with evidence from texts. Limited attempts to ask questions, build on ideas shared, or make connections.	Participates in a range of collaborative discussions with diverse partners. Comes to discussions prepared. Draws on that preparation by referring to evidence from texts. Attempts to drive conversations forward by asking questions, building on ideas shared, and inviting quieter voices into the conversation. Responds to diverse perspectives, summarizes points, and makes connections. Makes eye contact.	Initiates and participates effectively in a range of collaborative discussions. Comes to discussions prepared. Explicitly draws on that preparation referring to evidence from texts. Propels conversations by posing and responding to questions that relate to the current discussion. Responds thoughtfully to diverse perspectives, summarizes points of agreement and disagreement, and makes new connections. Makes eye contact and speaks loud enough to be heard. Leans in and actively listens.

FIGURE 8.6 Single Skill Rubric Template

1 BEGINNING	2 DEVELOPING	3 PROFICIENT	4 MASTERY

 Resource available to download at **resources.corwin.com/balancewithBL**

Ultimately, rubrics can make assessments an opportunity for students to learn. They help to clarify how students are progressing in relation to specific skills. By using descriptive multi-skill and single-skill rubrics, teachers can make expectations clear and decrease student anxiety around the grading process. In addition, narrowing the scope of assessment to a handful, or even a single, criteria can make processing assessment scores more manageable for students.

BOOK STUDY QUESTIONS

1. Do you currently use rubrics? If so, what do your rubrics look like? What scale do you typically use? Do you include descriptions of what each criterion looks like at different levels of mastery? If you do not use rubrics, why not?

2. How might providing students with rubrics at the start of an assignment that will be assessed impact their ability to be successful? What routines can you implement to help students explore and use rubrics?

3. Do you have students assess their own work? If so, how do you structure that process? How might asking them to assess their work using the rubric impact the quality of their work?

4. How can using rubrics with students support their reflective practice and help them to develop metacognitive skills? How can you use rubrics to encourage students to think about their learning and progress?

5. What do you think about the idea that you do <u>not</u> need to grade every criterion on a multi-skill rubric every time you assess student work? How might strategically selecting three criteria make assessing student work more manageable, both for you and your students?

6. What are your thoughts on the single-skill rubric? Can you imagine using single-skill rubrics for formative and/or summative assessments? Would focusing on one skill allow you to move assessments into the classroom?

7. How can using rubrics to support students as they work encourage self-assessment and drive reflection and metacognition help to support the partnership model presented in Chapter 2?

CHAPTER 9

Side-by-Side Assessments

"The word 'assessment' comes from the Latin verb 'assidere,' meaning 'to sit with.' The word origin implies that in assessment the teacher sits with the learner and assessment is something teachers do with and for students rather than to students."

— Margaret Heritage

Yesterday, I had a coaching session with a woman who teaches seventh-grade English language arts. She is in her fourth year of teaching, and she is exhausted. At the start of our coaching session, she confessed that she was struggling. "This just isn't what I thought I was signing up for when I became a teacher." She had heard me speak the year before and said she could relate to my journey. I had described my own exhaustion and disillusionment and how I almost quit teaching before deciding to embrace blended learning.

I meet a lot of teachers who are in moments of crisis in their careers. Their jobs are demanding. They feel frustrated by what they perceive as student apathy, they are drowning in work, and the time they invest in grading does not have a dramatic impact on student performance. This is a problem. Teachers need to embrace new teaching strategies that help them to do this challenging job in ways that are sustainable and rewarding.

ASK YOURSELF, WHY AM I GRADING THIS?

I need to begin this chapter with a disclaimer. Moving assessment into the classroom is doable, but it requires that teachers take a close look at what they are grading and why. If teachers are putting points on everything students touch to motivate them to do the work, the strategy I describe in this chapter *will not* work. Instead, I encourage teachers to ask themselves, "Why am I grading this?" The answer to this simple question can help to clarify the actual purpose of assignments and help teachers decide when, where, and how to invest their time and energy.

Some teachers may argue that it's important to grade everything because otherwise, students won't do the work. I disagree. I believe that slapping points on every assignment, which is incredibly time-consuming, is counterproductive. It robs students of opportunities to practice and fail without being penalized, and it robs teachers of time. There are only so many hours in the day and teachers should be intentional about how they spend their valuable time. The flowchart pictured in Figure 9.1 is how I approach feedback and assessment.

If the purpose of work is to practice a skill or review a concept, then I do not provide feedback on that work or spend time grading it. Instead, I might provide an answer key or exemplar, pair students up, and ask them to work collaboratively to correct their work and capture any questions they have about that work. Too often students are penalized for making mistakes on assignments that are designed to help them develop and refine their skills before an assessment. If teachers assign homework or in-class assignments with the goal of helping students to practice, I don't think that work should receive a grade that goes into a grade book. Teachers can put a check in the grade book to communicate to parents that students are completing the assigned work, but I don't think students should be graded on the accuracy of their practice. The goal of that work should be to help students develop a skill or learn the material and for teachers to identify gaps so they can be

FIGURE 9.1 "What Is the Purpose of Work" Flowchart

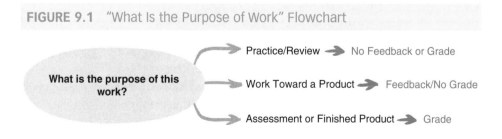

addressed. Mistakes during practice should be celebrated as part of the learning process. If we penalize students who make mistakes while practicing a skill, we create an environment where mistakes are scary. This can negatively impact student motivation and cause them unnecessary anxiety.

When students are working toward a finished product that will be assessed and receive a grade, they need feedback and support. If teachers create time in class to provide feedback, as described in Chapter 7, they shift the focus from the product to the process. Too often, students do not receive feedback until they have submitted a finished product and receive a grade. Feedback on a finished product is not nearly as useful to students as the feedback they receive while they are working. I encourage teachers to embrace their role as coaches in the classroom and invest energy supporting students as they work. This investment will help students feel more confident in their ability to be successful and yield stronger products.

FIGURE 9.2 What Is the Purpose of Work and Where Should Teachers Invest Their Time?

WHAT IS THE PURPOSE OF THIS WORK?	WHAT WILL I DO?	WHY?
Practice/Review	No feedback or grade	If students are practicing a skill or reviewing a concept or information that you plan to assess in the future, you can: 1. Give students time to self-assess using an exemplar and rubric or a grading key. 2. Pair students up and have them assess each other's work. Option: Extend the self-assessment or peer-assessment activity with a short written reflection asking students to reflect on what they did well, what they struggled with, what they learned, and what they need help with.
Work Toward a Product	Feedback/ No Grade	If students are completing work toward a product (finish a paragraph for an essay, write a draft of a formal lab report, or complete a part of a project), make time in class to provide students with feedback on their work so they can make improvements before the final product is submitted for a grade.
Assessment or Finished Product	Grade	If students are demonstrating their skills on an assessment or product (quiz, test, essay, lab report, research paper, speech), use a clear rubric to provide a grade or score on specific skills. I recommend creating and sharing rubrics before you assess student work so they know how you plan to assess their work. Then select two to three skills to focus on evaluating and provide an individual score for each skill. *If it is a finished product that students will not continue to improve, I do not provide additional feedback beyond the rubric scores.

Assessments and finished products need a grade, but many teachers either grade holistically so students are unsure why they received the grade they got, or they use rubrics composed of so many criteria that grading a finished product takes weeks. In this chapter, we will explore how teachers can shift the grading of finished products into the classroom, so they are not taking that work home to grade in isolation and passing back work with a grade students don't understand.

The more time I spend in education, the more I have come to embrace the mantra "less is more." By grading less, we may actually give our students and ourselves more. The more time we spend grading work that doesn't fall into the category of assessment or finished product, the less time we have to provide feedback, design engaging lessons, and recharge physically, mentally, and emotionally at home.

> By grading less, we may actually give our students and ourselves more.

At the start of my coaching session with Katee, the seventh-grade English teacher I mentioned at the start of this chapter, I asked her to tell me about her classes, student population, curriculum, and what she wanted to focus on during our 2-hour lesson planning session. After telling me about her classes, she told me that her students had just finished an argumentative essay. She was planning to take the students to the library at the end of the week to print out their essays so she could take them home over her 2-week spring break. She said her goal was to grade 10 a day, so she could get through them all over break. My response was immediate. "Why would you print them all out?" She explained that she liked grading on paper better than grading online.

I asked, "Are you planning to make notes on their papers?"

She looked a little confused, "Of course."

I asked, "Are they going to revise and resubmit them once you pass them back?"

She said, "No. This is the end."

"If they are not going to take your feedback and make improvements, then why would you spend your time writing on their finished drafts?"

She looked at me for a beat.

I said, "How would you feel about trying side-by-side assessments? If you grade those essays in class, you won't have to take them home and grade them over spring break.

Her eyes lit up. "Sure!"

My favorite moments in coaching are when I get to work with teachers who are willing to take risks and try something new. I could tell Katee was nervous about how to execute the side-by-side assessments, so I walked her through the process.

SELECT A BLENDED LEARNING MODEL AND DESIGN YOUR LESSON

To successfully conduct side-by-side assessments where the teacher sits next to individual students and grades their work, they need to design a dynamic, student-centered lesson that does not require them to be an active participant. This is why it is critical that teachers have already begun using blended learning models and believe that students of all ages are capable of learning on their own and with their peers. The teachers who still spend large chunks of class time at the front of the room explaining, instructing, and directing struggle to understand how a teacher can spend an entire class period (or multiple class periods) sitting off to the side of the room having conversations with students. It's hard for them to imagine learning that is student centered and student driven. When I've talked about this strategy on Twitter, there are always a few teachers who respond, "What are the kids doing while this is happening?" My answer? They are engaged, and they are learning.

There are several models that teachers can use to make time for side-by-side assessments. My personal favorites are the Playlist Model, where students are self-pacing through a personalized playlist of activities, or the Station Rotation Model that does not include a teacher-led station. When I was working with Katee, she had already designed and facilitated several Station Rotation lessons. Since she and her students were already comfortable with that model, we decided to design a 2-day, 4-station rotation in which students would spend 25 minutes in each station. The stations we designed are pictured in Figure 9.3.

As we designed the four-station rotation, I was focused on balancing online and offline work. I always recommend that teachers have students rotate between online and offline tasks, so they get a break from their computer screens. Keeping the tasks varied—online, offline, individual, collaborative—helps to keep kids interested and engaged.

After designing the four stations, Katee wrote explicit directions for each group to ensure that the students could navigate the tasks without needing to interrupt her as she conducted her side-by-side assessments. She also organized all of the supplies students would need at each station. Planning a blended lesson, writing clear directions, and setting up the room so students can lead their learning without needing the teacher is critical in making sure that your side-by-side assessments will run smoothly.

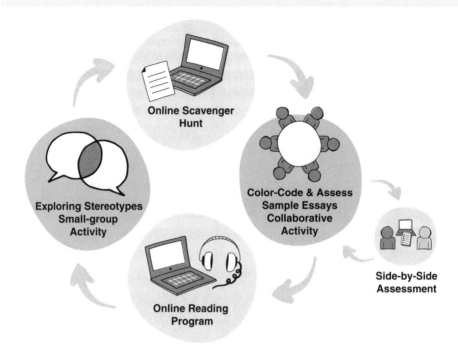

SELECT SPECIFIC GRADING CRITERIA FOR YOUR SIDE-BY-SIDE ASSESSMENTS

The biggest challenge I encounter when I am coaching teachers who are trying side-by-side assessments for the first time is getting them to limit the scope of their grading. Teachers feel immense pressure to grade every single aspect of an assignment. However, if side-by-side assessments are going to work, teachers have to be selective about what they are grading.

First, these sessions need to be quick. If teachers try to cover too much or grade everything, these sessions will require too much time. Second, students can only process so much feedback. I cringe when I think back to the start of my teaching career when I literally covered my students' papers in edits, corrections, and suggestions. It must have been overwhelming for kids to try to navigate all of that feedback. I've come to believe that limiting feedback to three specific skills or criteria makes these conversations more effective because students will walk away with a few clear, actionable items they can work on.

When I asked Katee if she used a rubric to grade her students' writing, she said her teaching team already had a rubric for argumentative writing. When I asked her what was on it, she said there were 15 different criteria on the rubric. I said that for side-by-side assessments to work, she would need to identify three or four skills from that larger rubric to focus on these conversations. She identified four skills that she thought were particularly important given the work they had done in class. I could tell she felt a little guilty about the prospect of leaving other items ungraded. I explained that narrowing her focus would help students have a better sense of what they were doing well and where they needed to focus their energy to improve. I repeated my mantra, "less is more."

PRIOR TO SIDE-BY-SIDE ASSESSMENTS, ASK STUDENTS TO COMPLETE A SELF-ASSESSMENT

I believe students should know how their work is going to be evaluated. At the start of any assignment that will be graded, I give my students the rubric I will use to grade their work. My goal is to make my grading strategy transparent so that students know what they need to do to be successful. A clear rubric removes some of the mystery that often clouds the grading process, as discussed in Chapter 8.

Giving students the rubric to reference at the start of their work is helpful, but I also want them to use the rubric to evaluate their work and continue developing the metacognitive skills as discussed in Chapter 4. Students need opportunities to think about, evaluate, and reflect on their skills and the quality of their work. Prior to a side-by-side assessment, students need time to take their finished product and use the rubric to score their individual skills. In addition to scoring each skill, I require that students write a short justification for their score. Why did they give themselves a 2 out of 4? It is important that they think critically about the quality of their work and articulate the reasoning behind a specific score.

The day before a teacher begins side-by-side assessments, I recommend building time into class for students to assess their finished product with a rubric. This practice helps students think about their work using the same lens their teacher will use when they grade them. It also gives them the opportunity to identify areas of weakness that can be improved prior to their side-by-side assessment. Another benefit of this metacognitive exercise is that teachers can note points of agreement and disagreement between the student's self-assessment scores and the teacher's assessment scores. In my experience, it is uncanny how accurate students are when they assess the quality of their work.

PREPARING FOR SIDE-BY-SIDE ASSESSMENTS

Below is the checklist I give teachers as they prepare for their side-by-side assessments:

☐ Set up a space in your classroom for these conversations

☐ Make paper copies of the rubric

☐ Decide how many minutes you'll spend with each student

☐ Get a timer

☐ Select a strategy for quick transitions

Set Up a Space in Your Classroom for These Conversations

First, teachers need to set up a space in their classrooms for side-by-side assessments. Ideally, teachers should position themselves in a corner where they can see the rest of the room. A two-seater, high-top table is ideal because the teacher has a better view of the room from the slightly higher vantage point. This table should comfortably seat two people since the student will need to sit next to the teacher for this conversation.

Make Paper Copies of the Rubric

In advance of the side-by-side assessments, teachers should pare down their existing rubrics to approximately three criteria. Then they need to make paper copies, so there is a stack at their table that they can grab and fill out as they evaluate each student's work. Since an increasing amount of work is done online, I find paper rubrics are easier to manage because teachers can circle the language on the rubrics that reflect what they are seeing in the student's work and make additional notes if necessary, without having to toggle between various tabs on the computer.

Decide How Many Minutes You'll Spend With Each Student

Timing is the toughest part of the side-by-side assessment. Typically, I recommend limiting these conversations to 3–4 minutes. This is challenging at first, but teachers get better with practice. If a teacher has 25 students and spends 3 minutes with each one, that is 75 minutes without transitions. If the teacher spends 4 minutes with each child, that is 100 minutes without transitions. If a teacher is working on a 50-minute schedule and spends between 3 and 4 minutes with each student, they will need to dedicate approximately 2 days to their side-by-side assessments. It's important to have a target time per student figured out ahead of time.

Use a Timer

Most teachers I work with simply use their phones to set a timer for each grading session. The timer helps the teacher stay on track, but it also provides a signal to the student that the time is up. If the timer dings, and the teacher is not finished, they should not cut the session short, but it should be a signal to speed up the pace of the grading session.

Select a Strategy for Quick Transitions

Teachers must decide how they rotate students through the grading sessions quickly without distracting other members of the class. For example, if students are engaged in a Station Rotation lesson, I recommend pulling students one at a time from an independent station. It's ideal if that station is close to the table where the teacher is sitting, so students aren't walking across the room to get to the side-by-side assessment. I also encourage teachers put numbers on the desks so students know what order they will be coming to the grade sessions in. For example, when the student sitting at the seat labeled number 1 sits down, the student at the seat labeled 2 automatically gets up to go to his or her side-by-side assessment. There are many strategies teachers can use, but they should select one and make sure students understand what is expected of them at the start of the lesson.

CONDUCTING SIDE-BY-SIDE ASSESSMENTS

Below are the steps I encourage teachers to follow during their side-by-side assessments to ensure they are successful.

- ☐ Set your timer
- ☐ Explain the process
- ☐ Think out loud
- ☐ Stay focused
- ☐ Complete the rubric
- ☐ Keep explanations brief
- ☐ Ask students if they have questions

Set Your Timer

When the student sits down, set your timer for your target time. Remember that if your timer dings, and you are still not done assessing the student's work, continue with the think aloud. Do not cut the session short, but the timer should be a cue to increase your pace.

Explain the Process

At the start of your first side-by-side assessment, briefly explain the process to the student. You might say, "I'm going to grade your work using this rubric. I'll do a think-aloud so you can hear what I am thinking as I assess your work. I'll ask you if you have questions at the end." This is a new routine for most kids, so it is important that they understand what you are going to do. As they get used to this routine, you will not need to explain the process every time.

Think Out Loud

The most powerful part of this strategy is the think aloud. As you review the student's work, verbalize what you are thinking. The think-aloud should:

- Point out areas of strength.
- Note when students have satisfied a specific requirement.
- Identify missing components and inaccuracies.
- Suggest areas that need more development, refinement, or improvement.
- Compliment areas of growth.

The think-aloud demystifies the grading process. Students can hear exactly what their teacher is thinking as they grade their work. Making our thinking visible can help students understand what they are doing well and what they need to work on. It is also an opportunity for us to model metacognition for students who will be asked to do their own think alouds to reflect on their learning.

Stay Focused

It's critical to stay focused on the specific elements of the student's work that you are evaluating with the rubric. For example, if a teacher has decided to evaluate the thesis statement, evidence, and analysis in a piece of formal writing, then he or she should not spend time talking through the introduction or mechanics. Focusing on elements of the assignment that are not being evaluated may confuse students and take precious time away from the elements that are being assessed.

Complete the Rubric

As you evaluate an aspect of the student's work, fill out the rubric so they understand the connection between your think-aloud and the scores they are receiving. In side-by-side assessments of student writing, I might say "This quote does not support the point you are making in your topic sentence. It's important that you select quotes carefully, so they strengthen your writing and support your topic sentences and thesis." Once I've read through the evidence students have selected, I circle the score I think best reflects their ability to select strong textual evidence. If they have heard me say that their evidence does not effectively support their points, then their score on the rubric for that skill will make more sense. As a result, there is less confusion about why they are earning specific scores.

Keep Explanations Brief

It's tempting to use this time to provide additional explanations and instruction because our instinct is to help students to develop. However, the purpose of these conversations is not to instruct, but to assess. As you evaluate the students' work, if you notice an area of need or specific skills that several students are struggling with, I suggest making a note for yourself during the transition time between students. At the start of each side-by-side assessment session, I write the name of each skill that I'm assessing on the top of a sticky note. If I'm grading an essay, one sticky note might say "textual evidence" and another might say "citations." If a student was clearly struggling with a specific skill and earned a low score, I write his or her name on the sticky note that corresponded with that skill. These notes help me to plan my lessons for the following week to ensure I offer additional instruction, scaffolds, and practice for students who need it.

Ask Students If They Have Questions

At the end of each side-by-side assessment, I turn to the student and ask, "Do you have any questions? Is there anything you want to ask me?" More often than not, the answer is "no." Usually, I have been in and out of their work multiple times giving real-time feedback, as described in Chapter 7, so they have had multiple opportunities to ask questions throughout the process. Occasionally, a student will ask for clarification or request additional help. If they ask for help, I add their request to a sticky note and make sure I carve out time to work with them after I finish the side-by-side assessments.

This routine of asking students if they have questions is a simple way to validate their needs and open the lines of communication. If the side-by-side assessment is simply the teacher talking without checking-in with the student, we are not nurturing our partnership with learners. They deserve an opportunity to ask questions or request help during this process.

Katee Dean
James Workman Middle School
7th grade English language arts
@DeanKatee

As I entered my fourth year of teaching seventh grade ELA, I found myself contemplating if this job was really for me. I worked so incredibly hard to get where I was, but couldn't imagine continuing a career like this. I was overwhelmed with the amount of grading I was taking home on a regular basis and the amount of family and personal time I was sacrificing just to get things done.

(Continued)

(Continued)

In early October, my district brought Catlin in for a professional development day. She said something that stuck with me: "I don't take my grading home anymore." I wondered how this was even possible and envied her for the simplicity with which she spoke about it.

Later in the year, Catlin was brought back for personalized coaching. I knew I could not let the opportunity pass me by. I had to meet with her. Of course, I asked her the question I had been dying to know. How in the world can grading be done at school and not be taken home? Her answer came in the form of the lesson we developed together: a side-by-side assessment while my students completed a Station Rotation lesson.

I was skeptical after our planning session, but what happened the next day was life-changing. Giving students real-time feedback and assessment scores on their finished essays was a totally new experience for me and my students. I could see them internalizing the feedback I was giving. They leaned in, nodded in agreement, and asked questions. There was something transformative about having these one-on-one conversations about their work. They were suddenly cognizant of the work they had produced. There were no secrets anymore. My students understood their grades because I was not taking their work home to grade in seclusion. Grading became a transparent process.

After conducting my first side-by-side assessments for 150 students over the course of two classes, I realized that I can work live grading into my lessons. I finally understood what Catlin talked about when she described the value of grading in class with the student sitting next to her. I haven't taken my grading home since that day. This experience helped to revitalize the passion I've always had for teaching and freed up so much of my professional, personal, and family time. Moving assessment into the classroom is the best decision I have ever made in my career.

Initially the appeal of this strategy from the teacher's perspective is that it eliminates the need to take piles of grading home. That's a huge incentive for teachers to try this strategy, but the real reward is the feeling of connection that teachers experience when they make time to sit with a student and talk through their work. Most students have never had this level of individualized attention when it comes to the grading process. Typically, students work in isolation and then submit their work, teachers grade in isolation and then pass back that work, and students are left to make sense of comments in isolation. Often, days or even weeks pass between when students submit work and receive their grades. This creates a disconnect for learners. The more time passes between submitting work and receiving a grade, the less invested students are because they've mentally moved on.

Side-by-side assessments can happen the day students submit work that needs to be graded. My hope is that by shifting assessment into the classroom students who have not been particularly engaged in school will lean into these moments because they are personalized. By making time in class for side-by-side assessments, the teacher is communicating that he or she cares about the students' individual progress and wants to support their growth.

BOOK STUDY QUESTIONS

1. How do you decide what to grade? What is motivating your decisions about what to grade?

2. Review Figures 9.1 and 9.2. How is this flowchart similar to or different from how you decide what to provide feedback on and what to grade? If you used the flowchart presented in Figure 9.1, how would that impact the volume of work you currently grade? What might be beneficial about using this approach? What might be challenging?

3. How can you use blended learning models to create time to conduct side-by-side assessments? Which blended learning models do you currently use? What modifications would you need to make to those models to ensure students could work effectively without you facilitating the lesson?

4. How do you feel about the idea of narrowing your focus when you grade to cover only a few skills? How might focusing on a few skills be beneficial for you and your students?

5. What is the value of having students complete a self-assessment prior to a side-by-side assessment? Besides completing a rubric and explaining their scores, is there anything you would add to the self-assessment activity?

6. Write a short 60-second elevator speech explaining to students the purpose of side-by-side assessments. Why are you using this strategy? What is the goal? What do you hope you and the students will get out of it?

7. What do you anticipate will be most challenging about conducting side-by-side assessments? How can you troubleshoot or mitigate this potential challenge? What protocols can you put in place to help these sessions run smoothly?

8. How do side-by-side assessments support the partnership model described in Chapter 2?

CHAPTER 10

Students Communicate Directly With Parents About Their Progress

"Communication leads to community—that is, to understanding, intimacy and mutual valuing."

—Rollo May

The expectation that a single teacher can keep 30–150 families abreast of their students' progress is unrealistic. In an era of digital gradebooks when parents can request a text message notification the moment a teacher enters a missing assignment, teachers feel increasing pressure to keep parents in the loop. I remember having a moment a couple years ago, after fielding a particularly angry email from a parent, when I thought, "How can I communicate more with my students' parents about their progress?" As soon as I asked the question, I caught myself. I paused and reframed. "How can *my students* communicate more with their parents about their progress?" As soon as I reframed the question, I began brainstorming strategies designed to increase the flow of communication between my students and their parents. This simple reframing exercise, which I described in Chapter 3, helped me to generate ideas for communication with parents that were sustainable because the student played a leading role in the process.

IT'S UNREALISTIC FOR TEACHERS TO COMMUNICATE WITH ALL PARENTS REGULARLY

I don't think the responsibility of communicating with parents should fall on the teacher alone. Students need to "own" the conversation with their parents about their learning. The student should be providing the parent with regular updates so that the grades are not a surprise. The goal of increasing communication between the students and their parents is to ensure that parents know when their child is struggling and needs help. On the flip side, parents enjoy hearing when their child is working hard and improving. There aren't enough hours in the day for the teacher to make sure every parent receives regular updates about their child's progress.

If teachers partner with their students to set goals, build metacognitive skills, provide real-time feedback, and conduct side-by-side assessments, students should have a clear sense of where they are in their journey toward mastering specific skills. In this learning environment, students should be able to communicate directly with their parents about their progress to ensure that their parents understand how they are doing in the class. Even young learners should know enough about their learning to articulate their goals and describe what they are doing well and what they are working to improve.

Technology tools make it possible, easy even, for teachers to support students in both updating their parents about their progress and sharing work samples so parents can see what their child is producing.

EMAIL UPDATES

One of the major benefits of providing students with real-time feedback as they work is that it's easier to keep track of who is completing the work and who is falling behind. Early in my career, I did not discover that students had not completed the work until a final draft was submitted. I always felt guilty entering a zero into the grade book for a large-scale assignment without giving the parents a heads up that their child was falling behind. Now, as I work with students in my teacher-led station or conference with them as they make progress through a playlist, I make sure parents are aware of students who are not completing the work I've asked them to do and which students are making significant strides in terms of their growth and development.

BALANCE WITH BLENDED LEARNING

When students arrive at my teacher-led station or sit down for an individual check-in or conference and they have not completed the required work, I ask them to write their parents an email explaining the situation. My students CC me and use a template, like the one below, to format their emails. I tell them that the purpose of the email is not to apologize, but rather to make it clear what they plan to do to catch up on missing or incomplete work. I want the students to use the email as an opportunity to think about what they need to do to be successful.

> Requiring students to contact their parents and take responsibility for their work at various checkpoints during the process of completing an assignment creates an incentive for students to prioritize their work.

This strategy is so simple and so effective! Students are rarely asked to take ownership of and responsibility for their work. Typically, a parent does not realize there is a problem until a zero is entered into a grade book or report cards are sent home. Requiring students to contact their parents and take responsibility for their work at various checkpoints during the process of completing an assignment creates an incentive for students to prioritize their work. This strategy also takes the pressure off of the teacher, who has traditionally been expected to reach out to the parents when there is an issue.

Dear Mom and Dad,

In [insert class name], we are working on [insert the name of the assignment]. I am supposed to be [target for the class]. Currently, I am [state progress]. My plan for catching up is [insert steps needed to catch up with completion dates].

Love,

[Name]

The most rewarding part of this strategy is getting to witness the conversations that take place between parents and their children. Because I am CCed on the initial email, parents typically "reply all" and keep me in the conversation as they dialogue with their child. I love the questions parents ask in their follow-up emails, like "Why weren't you able to complete this part of the assignment when it was due? How are you using your class time? What can I do at home to help you get caught up?" There is value in encouraging students to have these conversations with their parents if they are going to become independent learners. As soon as I adopted this strategy, more students completed their work on time, and several parents thanked me for keeping them in the loop about their child's progress, or lack thereof.

As more and more emails went home about missing or incomplete work, I decided I wanted to expand my use of this strategy to include positive updates. There are so many moments when I am working with students and see significant growth and improvement. In those moments, I wanted to create a routine where students would pause and email their parents to share their success. I created a series of positive email templates, like the one below, for students to use when they email their parents about their progress or growth.

Dear Mom and Dad,

Today I had a real-time feedback session with Mrs. Tucker. She asked me to send you an update on my progress. I've demonstrated significant growth in [state specific skill/area]. My work shows [describe progress and specific evidence of growth]. I plan to continue [state next steps for growth OR new area of focus].

Love,

[Name]

A couple of things are happening in this email. First, I hope that parents will read the phrase "real-time feedback session" and ask their students what that is. I know some of our class routines are unique. I hope that by including language about what is happening in class, it will inspire a conversation between the parents and their children about our class. Second, the student must describe his or her growth in relation to a specific skill or area of focus. This is an opportunity to put the metacognitive skills we have been honing to work by describing their development and progress. Finally, the student must end by either identifying additional steps he or she can take to continue improving this specific skill or identify a new area of focus. This directly ties back to the work students do setting and monitoring their goals.

Mr. Nicholas A. Emmanuele
English Teacher and Department Chair
McDowell Intermediate High School
@NAEmmanuele

Inspired by Catlin's procedures on having students update parents on missing work, I decided I wanted students to keep their parents or guardians updated more often on their progress. At the beginning of each semester, my co-teachers (Special Education teacher, Mr. Daniel Wirley, and Gifted Support teacher, Mrs. Jill White) and I begin by having students compose and send e-mails home once every three or four weeks. Parents are the recipients and my co-teachers and I are CC'd (as well as any Special Education or Gifted Education case managers, guidance counselors, or coaches).

A half hour of class time is normally sufficient for students to reflect once they are accustomed to the process. We provide a Google Doc template to our students that include the following:

Subject Heading

Salutation: *This can be edited with whatever the student calls his or her parents: one of my favorites so far has been a "Parental Unit."*

Note from Teachers: *At the suggestion of my English teacher colleague Mrs. Stacey Hetrick, we've begun asking questions for parents to "Reply All" to: What is a story from your freshmen year of high school? How do you cope with stress? What words of advice can you offer your student?*

Prompts for Reflection: *These include learning targets we're working toward, reflections on major projects, or even a further debrief on class discussions.*

Closing Line: *We often provide options of "Sincerely" or "Love," but some students adjust it to "Your Favorite Child" or something else that fits their familial relationships, whether formal or playful.*

Post-script: *This allows us, teachers, to include any brief notes on the curriculum or upcoming events or deadlines.*

The parental response (even when not elicited!) has been extremely positive, and this has served to empower our students' voices and bolster home–school relationships. I have also had students type in English and their home language. This process allows some parent–child relationships to shine in reading responses, but it has also built some meaningful connections. One father reported that he did not know his son could communicate his feelings until he read an email!

PUBLISHING STUDENT WORK

Often the work students do and the progress they make isn't visible to parents. Technology can bridge the gap between home and school. Teachers can leverage technology tools to make work visible to parents and provide students with an authentic audience, which is the best incentive we can give them to do high-quality work. If the teacher is the only audience for student work, that puts a lot of pressure on the teacher to provide all of the feedback. Engaging parents in this process can ensure students receive feedback from multiple sources.

Digital Portfolios

Younger students can share work with their parents using the digital portfolio tools that already exist in popular education tools, like Seesaw or Class

Dojo. Students can share photos, videos, drawings, digital files, and journal entries with parents using these technology tools. The ability to upload photos and videos of student work provides a window into the classroom that most parents don't get until Back-to-School Night or Open House. With a digital portfolio, students can share a steady stream of their work with parents and family members.

I've worked as a blended learning coach in classrooms where the teacher will remind students to make sure their work is "Seesaw worthy," which highlights the power of having an audience. If students are working on something that will be posted online where their parents and family members can see and comment on it, then kids want that work to be *good*. It is also helpful for teachers to allow students the opportunity to select a piece from the week that they are excited to publish. This gives them agency as they choose what they *want* to share with their families.

When students post work to Seesaw or Class Dojo, the teacher can review it before it can be viewed by families. When work is shared via one of these tools, families receive a notification via text or email alerting them to new student work. Teachers can message parents directly, and parents can respond to their child's work using voice or text comments inside of these platforms. This functions to extend the partnership around learning to include families who can support students after they leave the classroom.

Digital Notebooks

At the high school level, my students create digital notebooks using Google Sites. They organize their Google Sites like they would set up a physical folder. Each page coordinates to a topic or subject. They also create a page that functions as a learning blog where they post their Goal-Setting documents (Chapter 6) and their Plan Your Attack, Learning Log, and Ongoing Self-Assessment documents (Chapter 4). This section of their digital notebooks is extremely helpful for me because all of their metacognitive work is in one location.

When students create their websites, as opposed to using technology tools with portfolio functionality built right in, I would suggest teachers do the following:

1. Create clear instructions for setting up a digital notebook or portfolio.

2. Provide students with time in class to create their websites.

3. Talk about privacy settings and what is appropriate to publish.

4. Add links to the students' websites on your class webpage or learning management system (LMS).

5. Make sure parents know where to find their student's work.

FIGURE 10.1   Step-by-Step Guide for Setting Up Your Digital Portfolio

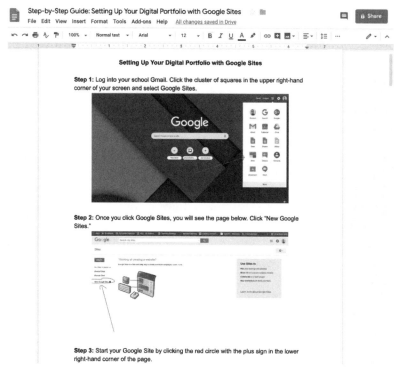

Source: Created in Google Docs.

Create Clear Instructions for Setting Up a Digital Notebook or Portfolio

I walk through the process of setting up the website before I have students do it. That way, I can create a detailed Google Document describing the process that students will need to follow. I break the process down into individual steps and include clear written directions and annotated screenshots to guide them as pictured in Figure 10.1.

If the directions for setting up a digital notebook or portfolio are explicit and detailed, the students can create their websites with minimal support from the teacher. Instead of leading the class through the process, the teacher can allow students to self-pace through the setup process, and the teacher can circulate to support individual students and troubleshoot technology hiccups.

Provide Students With Time in Class to Create Their Websites

Even though many students are proficient users of technology, some students are not used to using technology for tasks beyond communicating with friends or engaging on social media. Setting up a website to display work is a multi-step process that requires time. It's also worth noting that many parents may not be able to assist their students if they are attempting to navigate the parts of this process at home. Instead, I would suggest that teachers with access to a class set of devices design a Whole Group Rotation in which the class is working simultaneously online to set up their sites. For teachers with limited devices, I would create an online station in a Station Rotation lesson dedicated to setting up their websites. That way, if students are working on setting up their websites in collaborative groups, they can ask one another for help. Students are the most underutilized tech support on campus. I encourage teachers to instruct their students to ask each other for help when they get stuck. If they cannot troubleshoot a technology issue with a peer, I encourage them to search Google or look for a YouTube video tutorial before they ask me for help.

> Students are the most underutilized tech support on campus. I encourage teachers to instruct their students to ask each other for help when they get stuck.

Talk About Privacy Settings and What Is Appropriate to Publish

I'm a big fan of publishing student work for an authentic audience, but I am not naive. I know there are trolls online who spend their days posting negative, and often offensive, comments on other people's work. I have never wanted to limit what my students share or restrict their work to the eyes of people within our school's domain out of fear. I feel too many people in education make decisions from a place of fear. That mentality limits what students can accomplish. That said, I want students to know how to protect themselves and limit who has access to their work. Most of my students opt to share their websites with anyone who might stumble on them. However, if a student feels strongly that they don't want to publish their work so that it is searchable, then they can limit who can access it, by sharing it directly with me, their parents, and anyone else they are comfortable with. That is the beauty of working with a website creator like Google Sites.

In addition to discussing privacy settings, we talk about protecting ourselves and our personal information online. It's important to remind students not to share their phone numbers, addresses, or other personal information on their websites. If they want to include a link on their academic website to a social media account, like Twitter or Instagram, then they need to make sure they are not posting inappropriate pictures or sensitive information to those accounts either. It's eye-opening to have conversations about privacy, personal information, and public persona with students. It is clear to me that these conversations need to happen more frequently in school. Students are using technology tools that many of their parents don't use. Without incorporating these conversations into educational settings, I worry that students will not make smart, informed choices online.

Add Links to Your Students' Websites on Your Class Webpage or LMS

Once the students have created and published the websites that will house their digital notebooks or digital portfolios, I suggest teachers create a list of websites on their class webpage or LMS. I typically type a list of first names with last initials and organize them by class period then hyperlink those to the students' websites. This makes it easy for the teacher, students, and parents to view the students' digital work.

Make Sure Parents Know Where to Find Their Students' Work

Parents will only check out their kid's work if they know where to find it. I send out an email to parents explaining why the students are creating their websites. I want parents to understand the purpose and value of the websites. I also include instructions for how to access their student's work. In addition to the initial email I send out, I also mention them at Back-to-School Night and in conferences with parents.

Each week, at least one of my stations or online activities is focused on giving students time to update their digital notebooks with their work and write a short reflection on their learning in the learning blog section. Online websites make it possible for students to display their multimedia work and reflect on their learning, which helps students continue to build those metacognitive skills we discussed in Chapter 4.

STUDENT-LED CONFERENCES

Two times each school year, my children's teachers send a note home letting me know it is time for parent–teacher conferences. Usually, the letter comes with a calendar where I sign up for windows of time that work for my schedule. When I arrive for my son or daughter's conference, the teacher has samples of their work laid out and ready to discuss. During the conference, the teacher walks me through my child's assessments scores and describes their progress in relation to end of the year goals.

These conversations are the rare opportunity I get as a parent to hear how my child is doing in school. Both of my children have performed well academically, but whenever I meet with my son's teacher, I get to hear about how he needs to work on "managing his behavior." As a teacher, I feel guilty when I hear my child is not a model student. I wish my son was present to hear both the wonderful things his teacher says about him, as well as the challenges that his sense of humor creates for the teacher during class.

I have always felt it was a little odd that the student is not involved in the parent–teacher conference. I understand that teachers may want a private audience with the parents to tackle tough conversations, but there are ways to invite students to participate in the process even if the teacher does not want them to physically attend the conference. I would argue that much of the conference preparation—selecting work samples and describing the student's progress—could, and *should*, be done by the student.

Actively engaging the student in preparing for the conference accomplishes a few things. First, students must think about their work and evaluate the quality of what they have produced to select work samples. Second, students must reflect on and think metacognitively about their work if they are going to describe what the work samples show about their progress in relation to specific skills. Third, it reinforces the belief that the teacher and the student are a team working together to prepare for this important conversation. If the students do not play a role in preparing for or conducting the conference, then their perspective on the class and their learning is absent from the conversation between the parent and the teacher.

Even though I understand why some teachers want to have a private conference with parents, I prefer to have the students lead this conversation if possible. They are the learner. The conversation is about *them*. As such, I think they need to have a voice in that conversation. Unfortunately, at the high school level, we are not given time in our schedules to conference with parents during school hours. So, 2 years ago, I decided to orchestrate student-led conferences during our school day. I invited parents to sign up for a timeslot that worked for them over a 2 week period. I planned my lessons so that students would either be working through a Station Rotation that did not have a teacher-led station or making progress on a playlist. Designing these types of blended, student-centered lessons freed me to welcome parents at the door and field questions at the end of the student-led conferences.

The letter home clearly articulated the purpose of the student-led conferences. I included the following explanation in my letter home to parents.

As we approach the end of the year, I want your child to have the opportunity to share his/her growth with you. The conferences will be facilitated by your student. Your student will be responsible for articulating his/her goals, explaining his/her progress, sharing samples of his/her work with you, and answering your questions about his/her progress.

The conferences will last approximately 15 minutes. These student-led conferences will take place during the school day, so there will be a lesson taking place in the classroom. I will be circulating around the room to answer questions and will spend a few minutes with each family. If you would like more time to speak with me about your child's progress, you will need to schedule a time to meet with me on another day.

Although I made it clear that the conference would be student led and taking place during class time, I could tell some parents had not read the letter carefully before they signed it. As parents arrived, I met them at the door and escorted them to the corner of the classroom that was set up for conferences. I reminded them that their child would be leading this conference and I'd be back at the end to answer any questions that their child was not able to address. As I walked away from the first parent, I could feel her eyes boring into the back of my head. I could almost hear her thinking, *Did this teacher just trick me into coming to school during my workday to have a conversation with my kid?*

I worried that the parents might resent being asked to come to school when they have other obligations, but as the first student-led conference continued, the energy in that corner of the room changed. The parent was leaning in, asking questions, and pointing to things on her student's computer screen. She was clearly engaged in the process. At the end of that first student-led conference, I rejoined the mother and son to ask if she had any questions for me. Her response struck me. She said, "Thank you for this. I had no idea he was doing all of this incredible work. He never mentioned that he had created a digital notebook! I've enjoyed hearing about his projects and assignments." A wave of relief washed over me.

This same scene played out dozens of times. Most parents thanked me profusely in person or later by email or text for organizing the student-led conferences. Some remarked on how impressed they were by the other students who were working diligently without my orchestrating the lesson from the front of the room. It was clear to me that the way students were working, collaborating, and learning in our class was very different from their experiences in school. Even though it would have been nice to have a week of half days so I could meet with my students and their parents, it was valuable for my students' parents to see our classroom in action.

In part, I attribute the success of these student-led conversations to the reality that most kids, especially high school students, don't share a lot about their time at school. When parents ask about their children's day at school, most are probably met with little more than a grunt or a cursory "It was fine." Most parents have no idea what their kids are working on. Student-led conferences create a space where students can talk with their parents about their goals, work, and progress.

PREPARING FOR STUDENT-LED CONFERENCES

Teachers can ask students to help them prepare for a parent–teacher conference, or they can have students prepare for and facilitate the conference. Now, for teachers who do not want to invite parents into the classroom for a student-led conference and are not given time in their schedules to meet with parents during the year, I describe virtual student-led conferences in the next section.

Regardless of how you decide to run your conferences—teacher led with the parent (no student present), student led with the parent, or virtual—students need support as they prepare for the conference. I created the student-led conference form, pictured in Figure 10.2, to provide students with a structure designed to help them think through their goals, progress, and work.

FIGURE 10.2 Student-Led Conference Form

Student-Led Conference Form

File   Edit   View   Insert   Format   Tools   Add-ons   Help   All changes saved in Drive

	Current Goals	
Personal Goals: 1. 2. 3.		Academic Goals: 1. 2. 3.
What steps are you taking to try to accomplish these goals? Is there any support you need at home to help you accomplish these goals? 		

	Growth Over Time	
Select <u>one</u> piece of work from the beginning of the year. What do you notice about your skills as you look at this piece?		*Select <u>one</u> piece of work from the last week. What do you notice about your skills as you look at this piece?*
If you compare these two pieces of work–one from the beginning of the year and one from this week–what do you notice about the changes in your work? How have your skills developed? What can you observe about yourself as a learner by comparing these two pieces of work? 		

My Most Challenging Piece of Work	
Why did you struggle with this piece?	
What skills did you use while working on this piece?	
What challenges did you encounter while working on this piece? How did you work through those challenges?	
What did you learn from working on this piece?	

My Most Rewarding Piece of Work	
Why was this piece of work so rewarding?	
What skills did you use while working on this piece?	
What challenges did you encounter while working on this piece? How did you work through those challenges?	
What did you learn from working on this piece?	

Source: Created in Google Docs.

 Resource available to download at **resources.corwin.com/balancewithBL**

I've organized the student-led conference form into four sections. The first section is labeled "Current Goals," which is an extension of their SMART goal-setting sessions. In this section, students identify three personal and three academic goals they are working toward. They also have to explain how they are actively making progress toward accomplishing their goals and articulate how their parents can help them to successfully achieve their goals. If parents know what their child is working on personally and academically, they can provide additional support at home.

The second section "Growth Over Time" asks students to select a piece of work from the beginning of the year and a piece of work from the last week to compare. The goal is to get them thinking about what each piece of work reveals about their skills so they can appreciate their growth and development. It's rare that students revisit previously completed work, but it can be a powerful exercise that helps them to *see* how the quality of their work is changing over time.

The third section "My Most Challenging Piece of Work" asks them to choose a piece of work they struggled with and reflect on it. This section encourages them to be vulnerable and think about what they learned as a result of being challenged. I've worked with so many students who believe that struggling with a piece of work is a bad thing or a sign of failure. They have a hard time recognizing how much they grow when they struggle through a particular assignment or project. However, when they are prompted to reflect on that experience, it is often the work that was most challenging that they are most proud of.

The last section "My Most Rewarding Piece of Work" encourages students to think about the piece of work that was most satisfying and enjoyable. Nine times out of 10 the piece students select is a project or assignment where they had the freedom to make key decisions about what they focused on or how they completed the task. Student agency is a powerful motivator. That is clear in the pieces of work they identify as being most rewarding.

Students need time to complete this form and prepare for their student-led conferences. If they are leading the conference, they will also benefit from practicing with a role-playing exercise where they lead a peer through their conference content. Students get nervous if they know they are in charge of the conference, so asking them to complete this form and practice leading a peer through their goals and work samples will help to alleviate some of their nervousness.

VIRTUAL STUDENT-LED CONFERENCES

Teachers may feel they are too busy to host conferences in their classrooms or may not want to ask parents to come on campus for conferences, so virtual student-led conferences are an alternative way to keep parents informed about their child's progress. If teachers want to have students record virtual conferences, I suggest following the steps below:

1. Communicate with parents via email, virtual newsletter, or text message to let them know that they will be receiving a video from their child who will be leading a virtual conference to update them on their progress in the class. Explain that you think it is important for students to communicate directly with their parents about their progress and that the virtual conference is an easy way to do that without requiring parents to come to the school.

2. Explain the purpose of the virtual student-led conference to the students. Make it clear that this is a way for them to use the metacognitive skills they've been developing to share their work and progress with their parents.

3. Give students the student-led conference form and time in class to complete it.

4. Ask students to create a presentation, Google Slides or PowerPoint, to display their work samples, so they are all in one place and easy to navigate as they record their videos. They will need to take photos of any physical work samples they created offline and upload these photos into their presentation.

5. Model for students how they can use a screen recording tool, like Screencastify, to record their virtual student-led conferences.

6. Ask students to record a screencast of their presentation so parents can see their work samples as they talk about them. *Note:* I encourage students to embed the webcam of their faces in the corners of their screens as they record because parents enjoy seeing their kids' faces as they present their work and talk about their learning.

7. Show students how to format an email to their parents explaining the purpose of the virtual student-led conference, linking to their video from Google Drive or YouTube, and inviting the parents to follow up with any questions or comments they have after watching the video.

I have used this strategy with students whose parents could not physically get to school for face-to-face conferences. Some parents can't get out of work or do not have transportation, so we have used video. The responses from parents who receive videos are filled with gratitude. They appreciate that their student took the time to walk them through the parts of the conference even though they could not be there in person.

Parents are an integral part of the learning puzzle. The more teachers can provide parents with a window into what is happening in the classroom, the more likely those parents are to be allies in the learning process. Parents love their children and want to be helpful, but after elementary school, there are not as many opportunities for them to participate in the learning happening at school. Students are the critical bridge to making this connection. As I said at the start of this chapter, teachers do not have time to communicate with every parent multiple times during a school year, but we can partner with our students and give them the tools necessary to share their work and engage in conversations with their parents about their learning.

BOOK STUDY QUESTIONS

1. Do your students communicate with their parents about their progress in your class? If so, how? If not, why not?

2. How could you adapt and use the strategy of having students email their parents? If you have parents without email addresses, how else could you encourage students to communicate with their parents?

3. If your students had to communicate with their parents regularly about missing or incomplete work, what impact might that have on your students and your classroom culture?

4. Write an email template or script for a student in your class to use to communicate with their parents about missing or incomplete work.

5. Write an email template or script for a student in your class that is designed to help them share a success.

6. What tool could you use to have students publish work either in a digital portfolio or a digital notebook? What are the benefits for the student, teacher, and parents when students publish their work online?

7. Do you currently hold conferences with your parents? If so, what role does the student play in preparing for or participating in these conferences? If you do not currently conference with parents, could you use the student-led in-class conference or virtual student-led conferences described in this chapter?

8. How can the strategies presented in this chapter (communicating with parents via email, publishing student work, and conducting student-led conferences) support the partnership model presented in Chapter 2?

CHAPTER 11

Grade Interviews

"The influence that was highest of all in Visible Learning was self-reported grades. Overall, students have reasonably accurate understandings of their levels of achievement."

—John Hattie

began this book describing what I believe are key problems that exist in the traditional grading system. I said that traditional grades

- Don't reflect mastery of specific skills

- Are used as carrots to motivate students to complete work

- Place the focus on the product, not the process

- Don't clearly align with specific skills

- Don't provide an incentive for students to revisit and improve graded work

- Don't require that students think about their learning

- Happen *to* students

Throughout this book, I've presented the case that teachers need to partner with their students to shift the traditional workflow, engage students in meta-cognitive skill building, provide timely, actionable feedback, and create transparency about the grading process. The strategies in this book are designed to transfer ownership of learning from the teacher to the learner. Ultimately, learners must be able to reflect on, assess, and discuss their academic progress if they are to become active agents who are intrinsically motivated to lean into the learning process.

Every chapter in this book has led to this moment: grade interviews. As much as I would like to banish traditional letter grades from education, I know most educators are far from that reality. Every six weeks I am required to give every student a letter grade. So, I had to find a way to rethink my approach to grade reporting. I had to find a way to engage my students—my partners—in the process of determining a grade that reflected their current level of mastery.

STUDENTS BECOME ACTIVE AGENTS IN THE GRADING PROCESS

As each grading period came to an end, I felt that the responsibility for thinking about the students' grades should, again, be a shared responsibility. I didn't want grades to be a surprise. I didn't want students to be confused about why they earned a particular grade. Ultimately, I did not want them to be passive receivers of grades. So, I decided to offer my students the opportunity to request a grade interview if the grade in the grade book did not feel like an accurate reflection of their skills and abilities at the end of the grading period. In truth, assessment scores are simply a snapshot of a student's skills at a particular moment in time. Students earn some assessment scores at the start of the grading period, but that does not mean they stop developing and improving. Yet, if I don't reassess those skills again in that grading period, students are stuck with those initial scores. If I simply report the grade that my online grade book spits out, which is an average of all the scores I've input, then that grade may not be a true reflection of the student's abilities at the end of the grading period. Given this traditional approach to grade reporting, it is easy for me to understand why so many students become frustrated and disillusioned with school.

> Assessment scores are simply a snapshot of a student's skills at a particular moment in time.

Heather Ellis, Social Studies Teacher
Westview Middle School
Longmont, Colorado
@HeatherLea303

Grading conferences are one of the most impactful changes I've made in my teaching practice. I just wish I'd done it sooner. To me, those one-on-one conversations are more authentic than grading papers in isolation and handing them back with marks and letters. Conferences prepare students for workplace situations and shift the focus to each student's learning, growth and goals, rather than letters in the grade book.

In my class, students keep track of their learning in each unit by attaching work samples, inquiry research, and reflections to an active portfolio document. I collect formative assessment data and conduct mini-conferences along the way to monitor their progress. At the end of the unit, students complete a formal reflection using a rubric to write about their achievement, effort, and contribution to the class. They self-assess and give reasons for their grade. Purposefully, we sit side-by-side and look at their portfolio and reflection together. Most of the time their assessment matches well with the grade I would have given them anyway, but in these conferences, they own the conversation about their learning. If I disagree, we discuss it, each presenting our reasons until we can agree on a fair grade that accurately reflects their skills and ability.

When I first made the switch, it was in the middle of a school year and students were leery of the new system. It took a few rounds for them to trust the process and realize that I was on their side. When I asked if they liked the new system, the answer was a resounding "yes!" One of my shyer girls shared that the reason she liked conferences was because she felt like I really saw her and the work she was doing. Ultimately, that's my hope for all my kids—I want them to feel seen and know that I honor their efforts.

Similar to the experience of Heather Ellis, my decision to offer grade interviews was born from a desire to rethink the status quo and the realization that I am fallible. I make mistakes. Students do work that I don't see or assess. I wanted to honor that reality. I wanted to give my students a voice in determining a fair grade. Although I invite students to edit, revise, and resubmit work, and I offer them the opportunity to request a reassessment if they are not happy with their scores on an assessment, I am aware that they do work that I do not always see or assess. I have students who continue to work, revise, and improve their pieces even after I have assessed them. Offering grade interviews does two things: (1) creates an incentive for students to continue improving their skills after their work has been assessed and (2) encourages students to advocate for themselves as learners.

Karen Cribby
English Language Arts Educator
Westview Middle School
Longmont, Colorado
@kcribby

In my middle school classroom, students engage in structured self-reflection every single day. Our classroom structure blends independent work with student-centered activities, which creates opportunities for conferencing to happen throughout the class period. I run two types of conferences in my classroom: learning conferences and grading interviews.

Learning conferences focus on learning, and there is no discussion of grades. The learning conferences are where relationships and trust are first built. Students who enter my class with low levels of confidence in terms of their reading and writing skills gain confidence during our learning conferences because they are using their words to describe what they're learning. They also have the opportunity to ask questions and seek help. Students who typically "get content" quickly are challenged to advance to the next challenge because learning is never "done." During learning conferences, some students want to know what grade I'd "give their work." I remind them that they are not learning for me. They're doing this for their personal success. I'm there to guide them. Students are empowered by this. They own their learning and ultimately their grade.

During grading interviews, we meet to discuss how the student's work translates into a grade. To prepare for grade interviews, students use the rubric for daily work and writing. They formulate a claim for their grade, use evidence, highlight their growth, their concerns, their questions, and their "ahas." They select exemplars from their work to reference in our grade interviews.

I start grade interviews by asking students how they're feeling about their learning. The less I talk about the grades, the better for their agency. I tell students that I can evaluate their output, but I can never know them as well as they know themselves. They need to explain what they grappled with, what they didn't like, what they loved, and what they are passionate about. Ultimately, they are in the best position to tell me what they truly learned.

Combining regular conferences with self-reflection and feedback has helped my students to take ownership of their progress, learning, and, ultimately, their grades.

APPLY FOR A GRADE INTERVIEW

As the end of a grading period approaches (Week 5 of a 6-week grading period), I build time into our class for students to log into our online grade program, review their current grade, and decide if they would like to request a grade interview. If students are concerned that the assessment

FIGURE 11.1 Grade Interview Request Form

Grade Interview Request Form

Once you complete this form, I will review your request and schedule a grade interview if you have made a compelling case and are committed to the grade interview protocols.

* Required

Name *

Your answer

Period *

Choose ▾

What is your current grade? *

Choose ▾

What grade do you think you deserve? *

Choose ▾

What additional work have you done BEYOND the assessments reported in the gradebook that you think demonstrates a higher level of mastery in relation to your assessment scores? *

Your answer

Are you committed to being on time for your grade interview and prepared with a clear argument and work samples from this grading period to support your request for a different grade? *

○ Yes

○ No

SUBMIT

Source: Created in Google Forms.

 Resource available to download at **resources.corwin.com/balancewithBL**

scores in the grade book are not an accurate reflection of their current skill set or they have done additional work beyond those assessment scores that demonstrates growth and development, they complete a grade interview request form. The grade interviews are optional. If students are satisfied with their grades, they do not need to complete the form. Other students may not have the time to prepare for a grade interview; if it's a progress report, not a semester grade, they may opt not to request a grade interview.

I created the grade interview request form pictured in Figure 11.1 using Google Forms. It asks students to report the grade that is in the grade book and the grade they think they deserve. It also asks them to explain what additional work (revisions, practice, online work) beyond the assessment scores in the grade book that they believe has helped them to develop their skills to achieve a higher level of mastery. These questions require a degree of metacognitive thinking and reflection. They have to articulate how the work they've done has helped them to develop specific skills. This is where the metacognitive skills they have been developing with exercises, like the ones described in Chapter 4, are invaluable. Without regular opportunities to think about, reflect on, and write about their development as learners, it would be challenging to complete this form and engage in a grade interview.

I review the requests and schedule a grade interview for anyone who has thoughtfully completed the form. In a class of 30–32, I typically have 8–12 students who will request an interview. The other students have decided that the grade in the grade book is an accurate reflection of their skills and abilities and do not submit a request for an interview.

Occasionally, I will request a grade interview if there is a student I want to meet with to discuss his or her progress. For example, I have had shy students or lower level students who think their grades are appropriate, but I have observed them doing additional work and have a hunch that they have made additional progress. In those situations, I request that they complete the form and prepare for a grade interview. Instead of being put out, most kids respond positively to my request. I make it clear that I have seen them working hard and would like to give them a chance to share their work with me.

PREPARING FOR GRADE INTERVIEWS

Grade interviews are a little scary for students. In the lead up to our first round of grade interviews, I heard a student equate the stress of preparing for a grade interview with the stress associated with preparing for a final exam. I was startled. I enjoy the experience of sitting with students to discuss their work, progress, and growth. However, for them, it was a totally foreign and frightening experience to have a conversation with an adult. My students did not have experience meeting one-on-one with their teachers to discuss their grades, so preparing to lead a conversation about the grade they felt they deserved in the class was stressful.

After hearing the comment about how nerve-wracking the prospect of preparing for a grade interview was for my students, I decided to share a personal story with my classes about an experience I had as a sophomore at UCLA. I explained that I had taken a class and received a grade that I did not think was a fair reflection of my work. Even though I was terrified, I made an appointment with my professor to discuss my grade. I brought my work with me and made a case for why I thought the grade I received was inaccurate. After looking through my work and consulting his grade book, he agreed with me and changed my grade. That was a powerful moment that stuck with me. I realized that I had to be my own advocate. Similarly, I want my students to be confident advocating for themselves as learners.

In an attempt to alleviate some of my students' fears and provide them with a clear structure they could use to prepare for their interviews, I asked them to structure their interviews in the same way they structure an argument for an essay or a debate. I hoped the parallels between argumentative writing and this grade interview would make them feel more confident in their ability to be successful.

Prior to the grade interview, I ask students to prepare their argument using the resource pictured in Figure 11.2. They begin by stating a clear claim about the grade they feel is an accurate reflection of their current skills and abilities. The claim must also include three clear reasons to support the grade they are requesting. These reasons must specifically reference the work they have done beyond the assessment scores in the grade book that they plan to highlight and discuss in the grade interview. For example, "I deserve a B in English because I revised and developed my *Fahrenheit 451* argumentative essay, I completed additional practice on NoRedInk to demonstrate proficiency of passive and active voice, and I have worked to improve the quality of textual evidence I use to support my points in our online discussions."

Once students have stated a clear claim with three reasons, they must think through each reason, provide documentation of their work so it is easy to reference during the grade conversation, and reflect on what each piece demonstrates about their growth. For example, if the student has gone back to revise, develop, and improve a piece of writing after it has been assessed, they will want to link to that document and capture screenshots of the revision history so I can see exactly what they have done since I assessed the essay. Then they will need to reflect on the following questions in the last column of the grade interview preparation form:

- What growth have you seen in your skills as a result of completing this additional work?

- How have your specific skills developed as a result of completing this work?

- What have you learned as a result of completing this additional work?

FIGURE 11.2 Grade Interview Preparation Form

Grade Interview Preparation Form

Claim: State the grade you believe you deserve in this class supported by three clear reasons.	

Reason #1 Clearly state the additional work you've done to develop specific skills.	**Documentation of Work** Insert an image of work, screenshot of online practice, or link to work online.	**Reflection on Progress** What growth have you seen in your skills as a result of completing this additional work? How have specific skills developed? What have you learned as a result of completing this additional work?

Reason #2 Clearly state the additional work you've done to develop specific skills.	**Documentation of Work** Insert an image of work, screenshot of online practice, or link to work online.	**Reflection on Progress** What growth have you seen in your skills as a result of completing this additional work? How have specific skills developed? What have you learned as a result of completing this additional work?

Reason #3 Clearly state the additional work you've done to develop specific skills.	**Documentation of Work** Insert an image of work, screenshot of online practice, or link to work online.	**Reflection on Progress** What growth have you seen in your skills as a result of completing this additional work? How have specific skills developed? What have you learned as a result of completing this additional work?

Below include any additional evidence you may want to highlight in the case of a rebuttal.
  •
  •
  •

 Resource available to download at resources.corwin.com/balancewithBL

The value of this exercise is that students must invest time and energy in the process of thinking about the work they have done and how it reflects their growth. It is a helpful reference when they sit down for their grade interviews. Students who are nervous or struggle to be succinct in their explanations need a guide like this if they are going to make a clear case for a particular grade in a limited amount of time.

Similar to side-by-side assessments, grade interviews take time. On average, I dedicate a single 90-minute block period to these conversations the week before my grades are due. To create time during class to sit with students for grade interviews, the rest of the class must be engaged in learning activities that do not require my active involvement in the lesson. Depending on what we are working on and my access to a Chromebook cart, I will design my lesson using one of the following models or strategies.

CHROMEBOOK CART OR 1:1 WITH DEVICES	LIMITED NUMBER OF DEVICES
<ul><li>Students will make progress on a playlist.</li><li>Students will work on a hyperdoc or self-paced lesson on a Google Document.</li><li>Students will complete a multimedia lesson using Nearpod or Pear Deck.</li><li>Students will work on a self-paced digital project (e.g., infographic, passion blog, or video).</li><li>Students will complete an online scavenger hunt activity while touring a virtual museum or researching a historical time period.</li><li>Students will update their digital notebooks and ongoing assessment documents.</li></ul>	<ul><li>Students rotate through a series of online and offline activities in a Station Rotation lesson that does not have a teacher-led station.</li><li>Groups of students will work collaboratively on a makerspace or STEM challenge documenting their progress with a single device.</li><li>Students will complete an offline writing and/or art project.</li><li>Groups will work collaboratively on a lockbox challenge where they have to work through a series of challenges to unlock a physical box or a Google Form lockbox with a single device.</li><li>Read and annotate a text or create a sketchnote of a chapter.</li></ul>

I set up a corner of my room for these grade interviews, so students have privacy as we discuss their grades. I also post a list of student names with their interview times, so students know the order of the interviews in advance. It is their responsibility to be prepared with their grade interview preparation form and work samples at the designated time. If they are unprepared, they do not get a grade interview.

CONDUCTING GRADE INTERVIEWS

Prior to each grade interview, I pull up each student's digital notebook so I can reference their work quickly during our conversation. I also ask that every student come to the interview with a device and a tab open to their digital notebooks, so they can refer to online work samples during the interview.

Then I call each student up one by one and use my phone to time the interview to make sure I can get through them all in the time allotted. I plan for 6 minutes per interview with 1 minute of transition time. If I have 10 students interviewing, then I know I need approximately 70 minutes. If 15 students have requested an interview, which is the highest number of students I have ever had request an interview in a single class, then I need approximately 105 minutes.

The grade interviews follow the format pictured in Figure 11.3. Students begin by presenting their claim, evidence, and explanation. They have 3 minutes to present a clear and compelling argument using their grade interview preparation form as a guide. After the first round of grade interviews are complete, students have a profound appreciation for the value of the grade interview preparation form. Students who do not spend time selecting strong work samples or taking the time to reflect on their progress prior to the grade interviews tend to flounder. By contrast, students who invest time and energy into completing a high-quality grade interview preparation form are more confident and convincing in the grade interview. Figure 11.3 provides an overview of the grade interview format and the time allotted for each part of the conversation.

FIGURE 11.3 Grade Interview Format

3 Minutes	Claim, Evidence, Explanation *mandatory*	Students make a clear argument for the grade they believe they deserve using their grade interview preparation form as a guide. They highlight specific work samples and explain how the additional work they have done beyond the assessments support the claim they are making about their desired grade.
1 Minute	Counterclaim *optional*	If I am not convinced that the work presented shows significant growth or I have a concern about the student's skills, I present a counterclaim.
2 Minutes	Rebuttal *optional*	If I counter, the student has two additional minutes to present a rebuttal. Students have the opportunity to present a rebuttal responding to my concerns and presenting additional evidence to support their claim.

Some students make a strong argument, and it is clear that they deserve the grade they are asking for after the first 3 minutes. In that case, the conversation is over, and I update their grade accordingly. If after the first 3 minutes, I am not convinced or I have concerns about the work students have selected and what it reveals about their skills, I present a counter argument articulating my concerns. If I counter, students have an additional 2 minutes to present a rebuttal. It is helpful if they have already identified additional work samples on their planning document that they can refer to in this moment. This is why it is crucial that they come to the conversations with a device and their digital notebooks open so they can quickly find work samples they can refer to and discuss.

Grade interviews are a powerful way to give students agency over their grades. This increased agency has a direct impact on the students' intrinsic motivation. Students realize they can invest additional time and energy into their work to develop skills and, ultimately, improve their grades in the class. That said, the grade interview process is demanding. Students have to request an interview, prepare their arguments and collect work samples, and overcome their fears and nervousness about sitting with a teacher to discuss their grades. My experience is that the majority of students will only request a grade interview if they feel strongly that they have made significant progress.

After conducting grade interviews over the past 3 years, I feel guilty about all of the years that I simply reported the grades as they appeared in my digital grade book. During our grade interviews, I realize my students do work that I am not privy to or aware of. Creating a space where students can share the work they have done that I did not assign, require, or grade is an eye-opening exercise. I want students to be so invested in their learning that they *want* to pursue opportunities to practice and improve without me "making" them. Grade interviews create an incentive for students to go above and beyond what is required because they are in control of their grades. They know that if they receive assessment scores that are lower than they were hoping for, they can change those scores and, ultimately, their grades.

Another observation I have made after conducting hundreds of grade interviews is that students who were used to earning high grades often overestimated their progress, asking for a higher grade than their work reflected, while students who were not strong academically prior to entering my class often underestimated their progress. I have had hard conversations with students who wanted a grade that was not supported by the quality of their work or the strength of their skill set. Conversely, on a few occasions, students have asked for a lower grade than I ended up giving them because the quality of work they presented showed impressive skill development. These conversations placed the focus on learning and skills, not points. Even though some students left our conversations disappointed because their grades did not change, I believe they understood why they earned the grade they received. They left knowing where to invest their time and energy before the end of the next grading period. There was total transparency about what they needed to work on. I also walked away from those conversations knowing exactly who wanted and needed additional support.

Carlyn Nichols
Seward Middle School Science, Culinary and Maker Educator
Seward, Alaska
@Scisamurai

Of all the personalized, blended, STEM, and inquiry strategies I have adopted in the past few years, grade conferencing has been one of the most rewarding. In the past, I had students assess their work before handing it in, but students weren't "reading" the rubrics, and there wasn't much reflection or critical thinking evident. They viewed the self-assessment as a "hurdle," one more act of compliance, and for some, it was one more barrier to success. Now, students meet with me in a one-on-one grade conference where they "defend" their self-assessed grade and reflect on what they are proud of and what they can improve on.

Most of the assessments in my science class are alternative formats like models, engineering challenges, and inquiry projects that require more reflective thinking, iteration, and student ownership. Conferencing with students is essential for student success, buy-in, and effective assessment when using these tools. I've found that a blended or personalized learning environment affords me the flexibility to meet with individual students every week, which has transformed my teaching. Students feel heard, appreciated, respected, and cared for when they have regular individual time with their teachers. Our 1:1 time serves many purposes: targeted instruction after a formative assessment, a discussion of the student's weekly goals, or a review of their latest project outline. I have structured my classroom to create time for individuals and small-group instruction. The payoff has been significant. One measure of success is the number of students turning in projects who usually never complete "large" assignments because they feel supported and valued.

All students in my science class must meet with me in a grade conference to receive a grade for their projects or assessments. The process has been successful with students at all levels, including those with Individual Education Plans (IEPs), and English language learners. Before the conference, students complete an editing checklist, peer review, and use the assignment rubric to complete a self-assessment. Grade conferencing forces a teacher to craft rubrics that are clear, concise, accurate, and student friendly.

I initiate the grade conference with questions like, "Why do you feel like you are a 3 and not a 2 or 4?" This prompts discussion of work quality, growth, and an understanding of the rubric itself. The quality of the student reflection is due in part to a consistent expectation of learning and work using a 1–4 class rubric that the students help to craft. Our common language and expectations make the conferencing more effective. Students lead these conversations. The students' self-assessment and reflection typically mirror my own. I find that most students have a pretty accurate grasp of their work quality and understanding of scientific concepts. When I enter the grade during the conference, most students beam with satisfaction and pride. It's the most immediate form of feedback they receive, which has an added advantage of increasing the number of students who chose to revise their work. Our straightforward and honest conversations about their products make revision more tangible and actionable for students.

The process of conducting grade conferences is not critical or punitive; instead, it fosters student ownership and metacognition because they must be able to articulate what they did, why they did it, and what they learned. The focus is on evidence of growth and learning. They have my complete attention, and students relish that time with me. The conversations we have are comfortable, genuine, spark teachable moments, and enhance our connection. For this reason, I find them incredibly rewarding. Together we are building their capacity as reflective and responsible learners.

It may seem daunting to find time in the school day for conferencing, but it is doable. It requires reimagining your class and committing to this individual time with your students. I make time for conferences by meeting with students (1) during my teacher-led station in a Station Rotation lesson, (2) during independent work time, or (3) during advisory or by appointment. When using blended learning strategies, educators must build the students' capacity to be self-sufficient and empower them to self-regulate, so the teacher can focus on the student with whom they are meeting. Teachers in a blended learning classroom must learn to let go, but the payoffs are significant.

THE POSSIBILITIES OF A PARTNERSHIP MODEL

My decision to partner with my students on their learning journeys has led to some profound changes in the way I design and facilitate lessons, provide feedback, and assess student work. The relationships I have formed with my students have helped me to gain immense empathy for them and the pressure they are under in our grade-obsessed culture. By rethinking what, why, and how I evaluate my students' work and encouraging them to take an active role in that process, I hope that I can alleviate some of their fear, anxiety, and stress.

In the traditional school system, it's easy to understand why many learners are disengaged. However, if teachers use blended learning models to free themselves from the front of the room and implement strategies designed to put students at the center of learning, we can give them the tools they need to be active, engaged learners.

As teachers partner with their students and think about learning as a shared responsibility and joint endeavor, it can have myriad benefits for learners. Ultimately,

I want students to develop more confidence in themselves and their abilities.

I want students to understand that their grades are a reflection of their skills, and they are capable of improving those skills at any time.

I want students to complete assignments because they are meaningful, interesting, and rewarding, not because they are worth points.

I want students to know that I am here to support them as they work because learning is a process and everyone needs feedback and support to improve.

I want students to be intrinsically motivated to revisit and improve their work because they feel like active agents in the learning process.

I want students to *think* about their learning and understand themselves—their strengths and their weaknesses—because it is only when students know themselves as learners that they will feel in control of their learning journeys.

The vision I am advocating for in this book demands a lot from the learner when compared to their traditional roles in education. Students cannot sit quietly in classrooms listening to teachers talk, passively consuming information, and receiving grades. The simple truth is that it is much easier and less demanding to be a student in a traditional teacher-centered learning environment. It is more mentally taxing to be a student in a student-centered classroom where a teacher has embraced a partnership model in which students work alongside their teachers to reflect on, evaluate, and track their progress. However, I would argue the experience is more rewarding for students.

Some teachers will worry about transferring so much responsibility to their students and others will feel it is too much work to ask of their students. For those who worry about adding to their students' proverbial plates, I challenge you to think about what other tasks or assignments you can replace with the routines described in this book.

Teachers are creatures of habit, and embracing a partnership model will require that we rethink our current approach to instruction, facilitation, and assessment, but it also necessitates that we rethink the volume and types of tasks we assign. My goal is always to "replace and improve" when I adopt a new strategy. Instead of adding all of the strategies described in this book to your existing repertoire, what can you replace and improve upon in your current practice? How might replacing an existing routine with one described in this book impact the way your students view their learning? How might developing the skills of metacognition, goal setting, and self-assessment serve students long after they leave your class?

I've coached in classrooms where the teacher begins class with a "welcome task." The students spend 10 minutes working silently on an activity, while the teacher takes roll and finishes administrative tasks. Instead of a review activity or quickwrite assignment to begin class, teachers could dedicate 2 days a week to beginning class by having students revisit and refine their goals, reflect on specific assignment in a learning log, or update their ongoing assessment documents. This is a simple shift that could have a big impact over the course of a school year.

THE GOAL: ACHIEVING BALANCE

Throughout this book, I've advocated for a shift in the workflow, responsibilities, and ownership of the learning. Not only is this shift beneficial for students, but it is critical for teachers who feel tired, disillusioned, and ineffective. By giving students the tools to actively engage in the process of thinking about, tracking, and assessing their learning, we are able to invest our finite time and energy in the most rewarding aspects of our jobs. We can spend more time working directly with learners—providing feedback, conferencing about progress, providing personalized support, and discussing grades.

My hope is that by moving feedback and assessment into the classroom and asking students to actively assess, track, and reflect on their learning that teachers can stop dragging piles of paperwork home to grade. I believe teachers would be happier, more energized, and more present if they spent their time at home connecting with their families and friends, reading a good book, working out, or just relaxing and recharging for the next school day. It is important that we strive for balance in our lives, and I believe blended learning can make that easier to achieve.

BOOK STUDY QUESTIONS

1. How do you think offering grade interviews can help you to combat some of the problems that exist with traditional grading practices? What impact might grade interviews have on your students' motivation?

2. How would you decide who qualifies for a grade interview? Would you allow students to request a grade interview? How would you streamline these requests? Would you require grade interviews for particular students? If so, who?

3. How would you structure your grade interviews? Would you model them after the formal argument format described in this chapter or would you modify this format? How much time would you ideally dedicate to each interview to ensure this practice is sustainable?

4. What types of lessons could you design that would allow you to conduct your grade interviews while the rest of the class works?

5. Write a 60-second elevator speech articulating the value of grade interviews to your students. What is the purpose of grade interviews? Why is it worth dedicating class time to them? What do you hope students will get out of the experience?

6. How do grade interviews support the partnership model described in Chapter 2?

7. What do you plan to try first? What strategy from this book can you implement in your class tomorrow, next week, next year? How can you use the "replace and improve" mentality to ensure that the changes you make now are sustainable?

References

Bada, S. O. (2015). Constructivism learning theory: A paradigm for teaching and learning. *IOSR Journal of Research & Method in Education, 5*(6), 60–70. doi:10.9790/7388-05616670

Barnes, M. (2015). *Assessment 3.0: Throw out your grade book and inspire learning.* Thousand Oaks, CA: Corwin.

Brookhart, S. M., & Chen, F. (2015). The quality and effectiveness of descriptive rubrics. *Educational Review, 67*(3), 343–368.

Deci, E., & Ryan, R. (1985). *Intrinsic motivation and self-determination in human behavior.* New York, NY: Plenum.

Deci, E. & Ryan, R. (1991). A motivational approach to self: Integration in personality. In R. Dienstbier (Ed.), *Perspectives on motivation* (pp. 237–288). Lincoln, NE: University of Nebraska Press.

Dweck, C., & Leggett, E. (1988). A social-cognitive approach to motivation and personality. *Psychological Review, 95*(2), 256. doi:10.1037/0033-295X.95.2.256

English, A. (2011). Critical listening and the dialogic aspect of moral education: JF Herbart's concept of the teacher as moral guide. *Educational Theory, 61*(2), 171–189. doi:10.1111/j.1741-5446.2011.00398.x

Friesen, S. (2008). *Effective teaching practices—A framework.* Toronto, Ontario: Canadian Education Association.

Gagne, M., & Deci, E. (2005). Self-determination theory and work motivation. *Journal of Organizational Behavior, 26,* 331–362. doi: 10.1002/job.322

Hattie, J. (2012). *Visible learning for teachers: Maximizing impact on learning.* New York, NY: Routledge.

Hattie, J., & Timperley, H. (2007). The power of feedback. *Review of Educational Research, 77*(1), 81–112.

Heritage, M. (2010). *Formative assessment: Making it happen in the classroom.* Thousand Oaks, CA: Corwin.

Heyman, G., & Dweck, C. (1992). Achievement goals and intrinsic motivation: Their relation and their role in adaptive motivation. *Motivation and Emotion, 16*(3), 231–247. doi:10.10007/BF00991653

Khatib, M., Sarem, S. N., & Hamidi, H. (2013). Humanistic education: Concerns, implications and applications. *Journal of Language Teaching and Research, 4*(1), 45–52. doi:10.4304/jltr.4.1.45-51

Kohn, A. (2016, February 21). *Why grades shouldn't exist.* [Video File]. Fiddlestick Productions. Retrieved from https://www.youtube.com/watch? v=lfRALeA3mdU.

Panadero, E., Tapia, J. A., & Huertas, J. A. (2012). Rubrics and self-assessment scripts effects on self-regulation, learning, and self-efficacy in secondary education. *Learning and Individual Differences, 22*(6), 806–813.

Papaleontiou-Louca, E. (2003). The concept and instruction of metacognition. *Teacher Development, 7*(1), 9–30. doi:10.1080/13664530300200184

Peters, B. & Kalb, B. (Producers). (2018, August 27). *Episode 018: John Hattie, Visible learning.* [Audio Podcast]. Retrieved from https://blogs.svvsd.org/vrainwaves/episode-018-john-hattie.

Patrick, S., Kennedy, K., & Powell, A. (2013). Mean what you say: Defining and integrating personalized, blended, and competency education. *International Associations for K–12 Online Learning.* Retrieved from https://www.inacol.org/resource/mean-what-you-say-defining-and-integrating-personalized-blended-and-competency-education.

Pink, D. H. (2011). *Drive: The surprising truth about what motivates us.* New York, NY: Penguin.

Pierson, R. (2013). *Every kid needs a champion.* [Video file]. Retrieved from https://www.ted.com/talks/rita_pierson_every_kid_needs_a_champion#t-449570.

Prins, F. J., Veenman, M. V., & Elshout, J. J. (2006). The impact of intellectual ability and metacognition on learning: New support for the threshold of problematicity theory. *Learning and Instruction, 16*(4), 374–387.

Sackstein, S. (2015). *Hacking assessment: 10 ways to go gradeless in a traditional grades school.* Cleveland, OH: Times 10 Publications.

Schraw, G. (1998). Promoting general metacognitive awareness. *Instructional Science, 26*(1–2), 113–125.

Schraw, G., & Dennison, R. S. (1994). Assessing metacognitive awareness. *Contemporary Educational Psychology, 19*(4), 460–475.

Sinek, S. (2009). *Start with why: How great leaders inspire everyone to take action.* New York, NY: Penguin.

Veenman, M. V., Van Hout-Wolters, B. H., & Afflerbach, P. (2006). Metacognition and learning: Conceptual and methodological considerations. *Metacognition and Learning, 1*(1), 3–14.

Wang, M. C., Haertel, G. D., & Walberg, H. J. (1997). What influences learning? A content analysis of review literature. *Advances in Education Research, 2,* 87–102. doi:10.1080/00220671.1990.10885988

Wiggins, G. (2012). Seven keys to effective feedback. *Educational Leadership, 70*(1), 11–16. Retrieved from https://www.ascd.org/publications/educational-leadership/sept12/vol70/num01/Seven-Keys-to-Effective-Feedback.aspx.

Index

Virtual student-led conferences with parents, 143–144

Visible Learning for Teachers (Hattie), 86–87, 98

Visual maps, 73, 73 (figure)

Vocabulary, academic, 32

Weatherby, Joanne, 51–52

"Welcome tasks," 160–161

Whole-Group Rotation Model:
  about, 26 (figure)
  self-assessment documents, 53 (figure)
  video instruction, 60–61, 61 (figure)

Wiggins, Grant, 95

Work in classroom, responsibility for:
  about, 30–31
  exhaustion and lack of time, 29–30

math homework, student-led workflow for, 36–37, 36 (figure)

math homework, teacher-led workflow for, 35–36, 35 (figure)

reframing, 31–32, 131–132

workflow, flipping, 32–37

written assignment, student-led workflow for, 34–35, 34 (figure)

written assignment, teacher-led workflow for, 33, 33 (figure)

Working toward finished product (purpose of work), 119, 119 (figure)

Written assignments:
  student-led workflow, 34–35, 34 (figure)
  teacher-led workflow, 33, 33 (figure)

YouTube, 65, 66–67

A SAGE Publishing Company

Helping educators make the greatest impact

CORWIN HAS ONE MISSION: to enhance education through intentional professional learning.

We build long-term relationships with our authors, educators, clients, and associations who partner with us to develop and continuously improve the best evidence-based practices that establish and support lifelong learning.

Helping educators make the *greatest impact*

Corwin books represent the latest thinking from some of the most respected experts in K–12 education. We are proud of the breadth and depth of the books we have published and the authors we have partnered with in our mission to better serve educators and students.

Also by Catlin Tucker

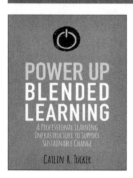

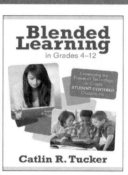

CATLIN R. TUCKER

This book provides a framework for leaders looking to implement a long-term professional learning plan that creates a "coaching culture" and supports teachers as they move toward blended learning.

CATLIN R. TUCKER, TIFFANY WYCOFF, AND JASON T. GREEN

Blended Learning in Action is the resource educators need to help them shift to a blended learning model and transform education for the 21st century.

CATLIN R. TUCKER

This guide helps teachers integrate online with face-to-face instruction to personalize learning, increase engagement, and prepare students for high-stakes exams without sacrificing class time.

CATLIN R. TUCKER

This road map to Common Core success includes specific recommendations for free apps and tech tools, step-by-step guidelines for meeting standards, and teacher-tested lesson ideas.

Also of Interest

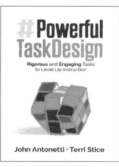

SERENA PARISER

This handy guide offers 50 proven best practices for managing today's classroom, complete with just-in-time tools and relatable teacher-to-teacher anecdotes and advice.

LISA WESTMAN

Full of step-by-step guidance, this book shows you how to build collaborative student–teacher relationships and incorporate student voice and choice in the process of planning for student-driven differentiation.

JOHN ANTONETTI AND TERRI STICE

This book will teach you to use the Powerful Task Rubric for Designing Student Work to analyze, design, and refine engaging tasks of learning.

JAYME LINTON

Designed to help K–5 teachers develop and implement a personalized plan for instruction in blended environments, this resource identifies key competencies and strategies for development.

To order your copies, visit corwin.com

TMN19C3